PLESSY *v.* FERGUSON

ourt Cases

v.

FERGUSON

SEGREGATION AND THE SEPARATE BUT EQUAL POLICY

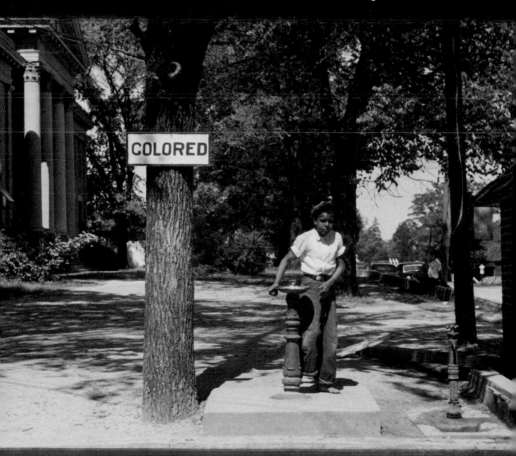

by David Cates

Content Consultant
Margalynne Armstrong
Associate Professor and Associate Academic Director
Center for Social Justice and Public Service, Santa Clara University School of Law

CREDITS

Published by ABDO Publishing Company, PO Box 398166, Minneapolis, MN 55439. Copyright © 2013 by Abdo Consulting Group, Inc. International copyrights reserved in all countries. No part of this book may be reproduced in any form without written permission from the publisher. The Essential Library™ is a trademark and logo of ABDO Publishing Company.

Printed in the United States of America,
North Mankato, Minnesota
062012
092012

Editor: Melissa York
Series Designer: Emily Love

Library of Congress Cataloging-in-Publication Data
Cates, David, 1963-
 Plessy v. Ferguson : segregation and the separate but equal policy / by David Cates ; content consultant, Margalynne Armstrong.
    p. cm. -- (Landmark Supreme Court cases)
 Includes bibliographical references.
 ISBN 978-1-61783-475-2
 1. Plessy, Homer Adolph--Trials, litigation, etc.--Juvenile literature. 2. Segregation in transportation--Law and legislation--Louisiana--History--19th century--Juvenile literature. 3. Trial and arbitral proceedings. I. Armstrong, Margalynne. II. Title. III. Title: Plessy vs. Ferguson. IV. Title: Plessy versus Ferguson.
 KF223.P56C38 2013
 342.7308'73--dc23
                          2012001279

Photo Credits
Farm Security Administration - Office of War Information Photograph Collection/Library of Congress, cover, 115; John Vachon/Library of Congress, 3, 17; Library of Congress, 9, 10, 41, 64, 70, 85, 89, 99, 104; North Wind Picture Archives, 21, 33, 44, 60, 80; Strobridge & Co. Lith./Library of Congress, 26; Bettmann/Corbis/AP Images, 53; Kean Collection/Getty Images, 56; W. E. B. DuBois/Library of Congress, 67; Everett Collection, 108; Russell Lee/Library of Congress, 113; Thomas J. O'Halloran/Library of Congress, 121; Gene Herrick/AP Images, 129; AP Images, 137; Bill Haber/AP Images, 139

Table of Contents

WHAT IS THE US SUPREME COURT?

The US Supreme Court, located in Washington DC, is the highest court in the United States and authorized to exist by the US Constitution. It consists of a chief justice and eight associate justices nominated by the president of the United States and approved by the US Senate. The justices are appointed to serve for life. A term of the court is from the first Monday in October to the first Monday in October the following year.

Each year, the justices are asked to consider more than 7,000 cases. They vote on which petitions they will grant. Four of the nine justices must vote in favor of granting a petition before a case moves forward. Currently, the justices decide between 100 and 150 cases per term.

The justices generally choose cases that address questions of state or federal laws or other constitutional questions they have not previously ruled on. The Supreme Court cannot simply declare a law unconstitutional; it must wait until someone appeals a lower court's ruling on the law.

HOW DOES THE APPEALS PROCESS WORK?

A case usually begins in a local court. For a case involving a federal law, this is usually a federal district court. For a case involving a state or local law, this is a local trial court.

If a defendant is found guilty in a criminal trial and believes the trial court made an error, that person may appeal the case to a higher court. The defendant, now called an appellant, files a brief that explains the error the trial court allegedly made and asks for the decision to be reversed.

An appellate court, or court of appeals, reviews the records of the lower court but does not look at other evidence or call witnesses. If the appeals court finds no errors were made, the appellant may go one step further and petition the US Supreme Court to review the case. A case ruled on in a state's highest court may be appealed to the US Supreme Court.

A Supreme Court decision is based on a majority vote. Occasionally one or more justices will abstain from a case, however, a majority vote by the remaining justices is still needed to overturn a lower-court ruling. What the US Supreme Court decides is final; there is no other court to which a person can appeal. In addition, these rulings set precedent for future rulings. Unless the circumstances are greatly changed, the Supreme Court makes rulings that are consistent with its past decisions. Only an amendment to the US Constitution can overturn a Supreme Court ruling.

Chapter 1

A Fateful Ride

On June 7, 1892, respected New Orleans tradesman Homer Plessy, age 30, boarded a train at the Press Street depot in New Orleans, headed for Covington, Louisiana, two hours away. Plessy purchased a first-class ticket, and he seemed no different from his first-class counterparts. Though it was a warm 86 degrees Fahrenheit (30ºC), he was well dressed in a suit and hat, according to the fashion of the day. He was calm and showed no signs of agitation or distress. Like the others in this whites-only car, Plessy was light skinned, and also like the others in the car, he seemed ready for an uneventful ride. But Plessy had no intention of reaching his destination.

This African-American man was forcibly removed from a train car in Philadelphia, Pennsylvania, in 1856.

This waiting room for African-American railroad passengers in Oklahoma shows the typically poor conditions of such segregated areas.

When the conductor for the East Louisiana Railroad Company, J. J. Dowling, asked for Plessy's ticket, Plessy handed it to him. Next, Plessy spoke words that would begin a legal struggle that affected the rights of millions of African Americans for decades and echoes still today. He said, "I have to tell you that, according to Louisiana law, I am a colored man."[1] And colored people were not allowed to ride in the first-class section of the train. Indeed, slavery had ended less than 30 years previously, and racism against blacks was strong in the South and the entire country.

Though Plessy was so fair skinned he looked white, it was true that by Louisiana law Plessy was colored. At that time, Plessy was called an "octoroon"—a person who had one black great-grandparent. There were many people of mixed race in Louisiana at the time, and the culture of New Orleans was such that the intermingling of races in public was somewhat tolerated. If Plessy had not spoken up, he would not likely have been challenged. In fact, a conductor could be charged with slander if he accused a white person of being black.

Though Dowling insisted Plessy give up his seat, Plessy politely refused. Dowling wanted Plessy to move to the Jim Crow car. This was a car of the train that was reserved for blacks, drunks, and smokers. Instead of the cushioned seats of the white first-class cars, the Jim Crow cars had wooden benches. These cars were usually placed directly behind the locomotive and were full of flying soot and engine smoke.

> " Be it further enacted that the officers of passenger trains shall have power and are hereby required to assign each passenger to the coach or compartment used for the race to which such passenger belongs; any person insisting on going into a coach or compartment to which by race he does not belong, shall be liable to a fine of Twenty Five Dollars or in lieu thereof to imprisonment for a period of not more [than] twenty days in the Parish Prison."[2]
>
> —THE SEPARATE CAR ACT, SECTION 2, ACT 111, 1890 LOUISIANA LEGISLATURE

According to Louisiana's Separate Car Act, the races were to be provided equal but separate accommodations on trains. Blacks were not allowed to ride in whites-only cars, or vice versa. It was doubtful, though, that any white passengers would willingly ride in the Jim Crow cars. The accommodations in the car reserved for black riders were very poor.

Eventually, conductor Dowling called for police assistance. An officer appeared quickly and escorted the peaceful Plessy to a local police station. This was all

SEPARATE BUT NOT EQUAL

In 1885, black leader Booker T. Washington described the inferior conditions for black rail travelers:

> On some of the [cars] the colored passengers are carried in one end of the baggage car. . . . The seats in the coach given to colored people are always greatly inferior to those given the whites. The car is usually very filthy. There is no carpet as in the first class coach. White men are permitted in the car for colored people. Whenever a poorly dressed, slovenly white man boards the train he is shown into the colored half coach. When a white man gets drunk or wants to lounge around in an indecent position he finds his way into the colored department.[3]

part of Plessy's plan. The officer had been tipped off in advance, and he was waiting for the call. At the station, Plessy was held for violating the Separate Car Act. Plessy spent the night in jail and was released on **bail** the next morning. His trial was set for five months later.

Homer Plessy

Plessy was born in New Orleans on March 17, 1862, and the city in which he spent his childhood was

bail—Money paid to allow a prisoner to be released temporarily.

different from that of his parents' time. He did not know the days of slavery before the American Civil War (1861–1865). Instead, he came of age hearing the ideals of Reconstruction, the decade following the Civil War during which Southern blacks enjoyed increasing equality and freedom. Louisiana desegregated schools in 1868, when Plessy was six, and in 1870, Louisiana's ban against interracial marriages was lifted. People of color began to be elected to powerful political positions. However, the promises of Reconstruction were soon tarnished, and Southern whites swiftly put in place new, restrictive laws that kept blacks segregated and powerless.

Plessy's father died in 1869. Two years later, his mother married Victor M. Duparts, a postal worker and son of a shoemaker. Duparts was an active member of the Unification Movement, which fought for civil rights for African Americans. At the age of 16, Plessy went into the trade of his step-grandfather, shoe making. Plessy came of age politically when he became the vice president of the Justice, Protective, Educational, and Social Club in 1887. By June 7, 1892, when Plessy would take his seat in the whites-only car and refuse to move, he was no stranger to the fight for civil rights.

THE JUSTICE, PROTECTIVE, EDUCATIONAL, AND SOCIAL CLUB

Plessy's Justice, Protective, Educational, and Social Club was dedicated to redressing the slights done to public education after Reconstruction. Immediately following the Civil War, the era known as Reconstruction ushered in an era of newly protected rights for African Americans. However, the Southern power structure quickly worked to reduce these rights. The desegregated schools of Reconstruction days, with their free textbooks and guarantees of equal education regardless of race, were disappearing by the late 1870s. In their place were segregated public schools so underfunded some had to be closed part of the year.

Club members were concerned that a lack of education would have far-reaching, damaging effects on children of color. The group feared substandard education would lead to ignorance and immorality, preventing the children from being effective US citizens.

The hearing for *Homer Plessy v. The State of Louisiana* before Judge John H. Ferguson began on October 28. A few scornful pieces were printed in the paper, but the trial otherwise began with little fanfare. But the case begun that day would take four years to resolve, moving from Ferguson's courtroom to the Supreme Court of Louisiana and ultimately to the US Supreme Court. Plessy's attorneys would challenge the

15

United States to uphold the promises of the amendments to the US Constitution that granted equal citizenship to blacks. Moreover, *Plessy v. Ferguson* would challenge the definition of race itself. Its resolution ushered in an era of legal racial segregation that would last until the ruling was finally overturned in 1954. ~

COLORED

The South remained segregated for more than half of the twentieth century.

Chapter 2

Slavery and the Civil War

efore the Thirteenth Amendment to the US Constitution was ratified on December 6, 1865, slavery was legal in the United States. This practice had a long and painful history in the country.

The type of slavery practiced in the United States came about in the seventeenth century, when the American colonies were still under European control. In the early days of European settlement, there were Africans in the colonies, but they were indentured servants. European indentured servants traded labor for passage to the New World. At the end of the agreed upon term, the servant would be free to go. African and non-Christian indentured servants were brought to the colonies against their will, but the indenture system allowed them to eventually earn their freedom. This began changing in the mid-seventeenth century.

Primarily to increase profits for landowners, Massachusetts, Virginia, and other colonies eventually passed **legislation** that made it legal to enslave Africans. In 1662, a law passed in Virginia enslaving the children of slave mothers, solidifying the system of slavery. Other states soon passed similar

> "From [slavery], there springs an unceasing stream of most revolting cruelties. The very accompaniments of the slave system stamp it as the offspring of hell itself. To ensure good behavior, the slaveholder relies on the whip; to induce proper humility, he relies on the whip; to rebuke what he is pleased to term insolence, he relies on the whip; to supply the place of wages, as an incentive to toil, he relies on the whip; to bind down the spirit of the slave, to imbrute and to destroy his manhood, he relies on the whip; the chain, the gag, the thumb-screw, the pillory, the bowie-knife, the pistol, and the blood-hound."[1]
>
> —*ABOLITIONIST AND ESCAPED SLAVE FREDERICK DOUGLASS, "SPEECH ON AMERICAN SLAVERY," 1850*

legislation—Laws.

laws. The Africans brought unwillingly to the colonies would no longer be able to work for their freedom, and their children would be slaves, too. Although Northern states gradually ended slavery around the turn of the nineteenth century, by the time of the Civil War, the South would have more than 4 million slaves.

Slavery was deeply rooted in Southern society. On one hand, slavery made the South more prosperous. With the late-eighteenth century invention of the cotton gin, a machine that quickly separated cotton fibers from seeds, huge cotton plantations became economically feasible. These plantations depended on slave labor. On the other hand, the majority of whites, in both the North and the South, believed they were superior to blacks. Many slave owners argued enslaving blacks was the best way to make them Christians and make them conform to white civilization. In that way, the cruelty of slavery was twisted in some minds into a social good. This racism cast a dark shadow after the Civil War.

Dred Scott

The importance and impact of the *Plessy* case cannot be fully understood without looking at the 1857 case

The invention of the cotton gin made slavery even more entrenched in the South.

of *Dred Scott v. Sandford*, in which the enslaved Dred Scott sued for his freedom. He believed he and his family should have been free because their owner took them to live in places where slavery was illegal. The case went to the US Supreme Court. This monumental Supreme Court ruling not only decided Scott would remain a slave, but also decreed slavery could not be challenged by Congress and denied any form of citizenship to slaves or freedmen.

Scott was born a slave in Virginia around the turn of the nineteenth century, though his owner soon moved with him to Saint Louis, Missouri. He was sold to a military doctor, Dr. John Emerson, and he accompanied this doctor to many different military posts. Some of these posts were in territories where slavery was forbidden by law. While in free territory, Scott unofficially married another slave. They had two children, one of whom was born in free territory. Dr. Emerson eventually moved the Scott family back to Saint Louis. After Dr. Emerson died, his widow, Irene Emerson, hired out Scott and his family to work in other households. The Scotts, perhaps because they were being hired out to other families or because their offer to buy their own freedom may have been refused, sued for their freedom on April 6, 1846.

After their first case was dismissed, their second **suit** resulted in a ruling that the Scotts should be set free, due to the many years they had lived in free regions.

Emerson and her brother John Sanford (misspelled Sandford in the court proceedings) **appealed** the case to the Missouri State Supreme Court, which overturned the lower court's verdict. Scott sued again and was defeated again.

This last defeat was appealed to the US Supreme Court, and the decision was announced on March 6, 1857. Although two **justices** ruled in favor of Scott, the other seven ruled against him. These pro-slavery justices used the *Scott* case not only to deny Scott and his family their freedom, but also to deny all rights to slaves and establish that any federal laws prohibiting slavery were **unconstitutional**.

Chief Justice Roger B. Taney found that states had the power to make their own laws about slavery. Slaves, according to Taney's ruling, were not and never could be citizens. And while some free states considered black

appealed—Petitioned a higher court to review the decision or proceedings of a lower court.

chief justice—The presiding judge of the US Supreme Court.

justice—A member of the US Supreme Court.

suit—Legal action brought against a party.

unconstitutional—Inconsistent with a constitution.

residents to be citizens, there was no national citizenship for blacks. Without US citizenship, blacks would not enjoy the basic civil rights of citizens, such as voting, owning property, and fair trials. This ruling heightened tensions between the proslavery and abolitionist movements and moved the country toward civil war.

> "[Blacks are] beings of an inferior order and altogether unfit to associate with the white race, either in social or political relations; and so far inferior that they had no rights which the white man was bound to respect."[2]
> —*CHIEF JUSTICE ROGER B. TANEY, SCOTT RULING, 1857*

The Emancipation Proclamation

Abraham Lincoln ran for president embracing the position that slavery should not expand into new areas. He was elected president of the United States on November 6, 1860. The Southern states were not happy with the election of Lincoln. On December 20, South Carolina seceded from the Union, to be followed by six other states in the next two months. The seceded states set up their own government, the Confederate States of America, with their own president. The Union was crumbling as Lincoln took up his duties.

In an attempt to lessen the frictions between the North and the South, Lincoln asserted that his main purpose was to maintain the Union, not to end slavery or change the laws pertaining to slavery. And when the Civil War began, many black Americans were turned away from the ranks of the Union army.

> " My paramount object in this struggle is to save the Union, and is not either to save or destroy slavery."[3]
> —ABRAHAM LINCOLN, AUGUST 22, 1862

As the war progressed, Lincoln came to reconsider his stance on slavery. The Confederacy had the advantage of using slave labor to build military installations, while the North turned away blacks who were willing to support the Union. Also, the Confederacy was close to gaining the support of European countries. Lincoln came to see a limited emancipation of slaves as a way to increase the workforce of the Union army and to sway European favor back to the Union side.

The conflict between the North and the South had raged on for less than two years when, on New Year's Day, 1863, Lincoln issued his Emancipation Proclamation. It declared,

Lincoln's Emancipation Proclamation freed many slaves. All slaves would not be free until after the Civil War.

All persons held as slaves within any State or designated part of a State, the people whereof shall then be in rebellion against the United States, shall be then, thenceforward, and forever free.[4]

In effect, Lincoln freed all slaves who resided within areas that were actively rebelling against the Union. The proclamation did not, however, free the slaves in slave states that were loyal to the Union—Maryland, Delaware, Kentucky, Missouri, and West Virginia. All in all, 1 million people were left in slavery in Union territory following the proclamation.

Ultimately, huge numbers of blacks participated in the North's victory over the South in the Civil War. Though the North began the war with no intention of freeing the slaves, the war could not have been won without the assistance of the 200,000 black soldiers who fought for the North as well as the 300,000 who helped with their labor.[5] These soldiers and other freedmen and slaves, though integral to the Union's victory, held no national citizenship and were not privileged to civil liberties. This injustice would only be changed by amending the US Constitution.

Civil Liberties and
Constitutional Amendments

The Civil War began as a war to keep the Union from splitting apart. But the war gradually came to include not only saving the Union but also freeing the slaves. But what rights would these freed slaves, as well as the blacks who had fought for their freedom, have when the dust of the war settled?

The US government established the Freedmen's Bureau immediately after the war and originally intended the bureau to exist for one year. The bureau worked to help the South transition from a slave society into one in which blacks and whites had equal footing. The bureau was to establish schools for freed slaves, make sure contracts between whites and freed slaves were honored, help freed slaves acquire land, and ensure blacks received justice in the courts. Though renewed through 1872, the bureau lacked the military support it needed from the government and made minimal progress in securing the rights of freed slaves in the South.

Meanwhile, the US Congress was working on legislation to secure the rights of freed slaves in the South. Congress passed the Thirteenth Amendment on

January 31, 1865, before Lincoln's death on April 14. The states ratified it on December 6, 1865. The Thirteenth Amendment abolished slavery, stating:

> *Neither slavery nor involuntary servitude, except as punishment for crime whereof the party shall have been duly* **convicted***, shall exist within the United States, or any place subject to their* **jurisdiction***.*[6]

While the Thirteenth Amendment abolished slavery, the Civil Rights Act of 1866 guaranteed the rights of all men regardless of color or race, whether freed slave or not. Congress passed the bill over the veto of the new president, Andrew Johnson. The bill also took a tremendous step forward toward establishing equality for blacks in the United States, granting them the citizenship that had been denied them by the *Scott* ruling.

Ultimately, two more amendments were added to the Constitution in order to secure the rights and liberties of the freed slaves. These were the Fourteenth and Fifteenth amendments, which were ratified on

convicted—Found someone guilty.
jurisdiction—The authority to govern or try cases; also refers to the territory under that authority.

THE FOURTEENTH AMENDMENT

The Fourteenth Amendment consists of five sections. Sections 2 through 4 concern war debt, voting, and electing new federal officers in Southern states. Sections 1 and 5 allow the federal government to protect civil rights. They read:

> *Section 1. All persons born or naturalized in the United States, and subject to the jurisdiction thereof, are citizens of the United States and of the state wherein they reside. No state shall make or enforce any law which shall abridge the privileges or immunities of citizens of the United States; nor shall any state deprive any person of life, liberty, or property, without due process of law; nor deny to any person within its jurisdiction the equal protection of the laws.*
>
> *. . .*
>
> *Section 5. The Congress shall have power to enforce, by appropriate legislation, the provisions of this article.*[7]

Section 1 limits the states' abilities to make laws that deny people's rights. Section 5 gives Congress the power to make laws to enforce the amendment. The framers of the Fourteenth Amendment intended for this amendment to give Congress power to protect civil rights from abuse by the states.

July 9, 1868, and February 3, 1870, respectively. The Fifteenth Amendment granted black men the right to vote. Women of any race would not gain the right to vote until 1920. The Fourteenth Amendment, however, would deal the final blow to the *Scott* ruling and **constitutionally** guarantee the citizenship of freed slaves. In addition, the amendment prohibited any state from depriving "any person of life, liberty, or property, without **due process of law**; nor deny to any person within its jurisdiction the equal protection of the laws."[8] It would be the Fourteenth Amendment and its guarantee of a federal citizenship that the *Plessy* defense would rely upon so heavily. ~

constitutionally—With respect to a constitution.

due process of law—A basic principle in the US legal system that requires fairness in the government's dealings with people.

Chapter 3

The Black Codes and Reconstruction

*I*n the first few years following the Civil War, new legislation had tried to protect the equal citizenship and civil liberties of blacks. But the situation was much more complex than simply granting equal rights to the freed slaves. And blacks would soon find themselves once again with little power and protection.

Under a New President

With Lincoln's assassination on April 14, 1865, Andrew Johnson became president. Johnson was a

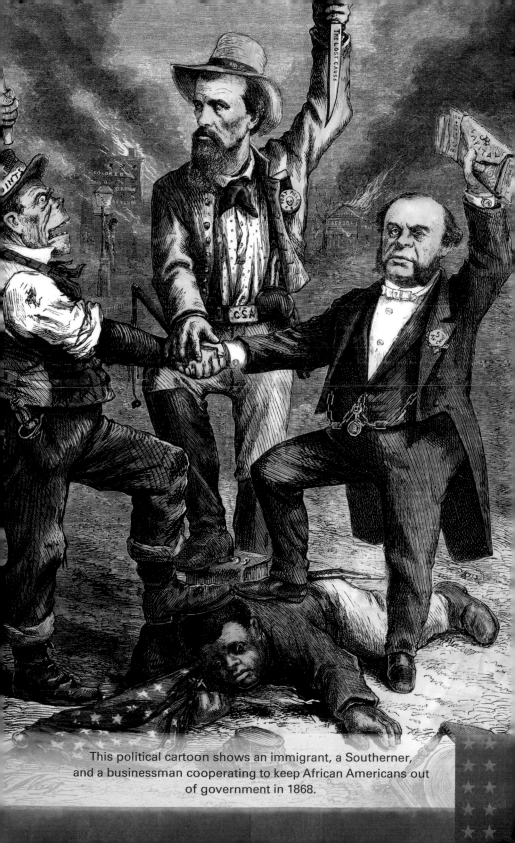

This political cartoon shows an immigrant, a Southerner, and a businessman cooperating to keep African Americans out of government in 1868.

Tennessean and sympathetic to the Southern cause, though he was pro-Union. Although Lincoln was a Republican, Johnson was a Democrat. Lincoln had chosen Johnson as his vice president to improve his own chance for reelection in 1864.

As a senator from Tennessee, Johnson had voted against secession from the Union. However, this was not due to any objections to slavery, but rather because he believed secession itself was unconstitutional. Although Lincoln's administration had set aside a limited amount of land for freedmen, Johnson's belief that "white men alone must manage the South" led him to restore ownership of land in the South to its previous owners.[1] Johnson began a rapid withdrawal of Northern troops, starting with black Union soldiers, and he pardoned those Confederate soldiers who would swear allegiance to the Union. Land and property were restored to most.

Thanks to Johnson's efforts, conditions were ripe for Southern whites to reestablish their oppressive system of exploiting Southern blacks. It did not take Southern states long to enact laws that limited the rights of freed blacks in an attempt to re-establish some semblance of the way things were before the war. These laws were called Black Codes.

THE BLACK CODES AND THE SLAVE CODES

The Black Codes were enacted between 1865 and 1866 as an immediate response to the abolition of slavery. They were based on the slave codes that had been in effect before the Civil War. The slave codes varied from state to state, but overall they enforced the institution of slavery. In the slave codes, a person was colored or black if he or she had any African ancestry. A child was a slave if his or her mother was a slave, regardless of the color or free status of the father. Slaves were not allowed to assemble, travel, marry officially, possess weapons, or learn to read and write. The Black Codes were modeled on the slave codes and attempted to maintain as much white control as possible over the newly freed black population.

The Black Codes of the South placed great limitations on the rights of freed slaves and in some senses practically re-enslaved them. These laws defined which people were considered colored. These codes limited the types of occupations black people could hold, limiting them to agricultural or domestic jobs. A black person without a job might be forced to enter into a labor contract or apprenticeship, or he or she might be forced to leave the area. Freedom of movement was limited for black people, as were their rights to own or rent property. The overall effect of the Black Codes was to oppress the freed blacks and provide the Southern

The politics of President Johnson versus the Radical Republicans was not as simple as white interests versus black. Johnson wanted a quick and easy readmission of the Southern states, which were heavily Democrat. This would give the Democratic Party control of Congress. In a similar way, the ruling Republicans wanted to slow the readmission process in order to enfranchise freed slaves. By giving the freed slaves the vote, Republicans figured they could keep control of Congress.

states with the cheap labor they had lost when the North emancipated the slaves.

Reconstruction

In response to the Black Codes and to President Johnson's sympathy for the South, in 1866, Congress passed the first Civil Rights Act over Johnson's veto, granting citizenship and equal rights to all males in the United States. Next, the Radical Republicans in Congress began passing the so-called Reconstruction Acts. Reconstruction generally refers to the period during which the North occupied the South after the Civil War. Initially, pro-South politicians hoped the reentry of the former Confederate states to the Union would be smooth and cost the South little. This was not to be. Though Johnson was sympathetic to the white Southern power structure, especially the rights of the average white Southern man, Radical Republicans ruled Congress. These men, for many reasons, wanted to punish the South for the Civil War. They also wanted to transform the racist South into a region of racial equality—on paper at least, if not in reality.

RADICAL REPUBLICANS

The Republican Party was created in 1854 and quickly became a major party in US politics. One of the party's early goals was abolishing slavery in US territories, and the first Republican president, Lincoln, abolished slavery throughout the entire country.

In 1866, a wing of the party known as the Radical Republicans took control of Congress. They were known as radical because they pushed for sweeping reforms in the post–Civil War South, and they were in favor of increasing civil rights for blacks. They wanted to punish former Confederates much more harshly than the Democratic president Johnson wanted to, and they held enough seats to overturn Johnson's vetoes. Indeed, when the Radical Republicans pushed for Johnson's removal from office, the measure was blocked by only one vote. During this era, the North was solidly Republican, as were freed slaves in the South. Southern whites were almost exclusively Democrats.

In response to the Black Codes, Congress passed four Reconstruction Acts between March 1867 and March 1868. Johnson vetoed these acts, but there were enough votes in Congress to pass them anyway. The acts put pressure on Southern states to adopt laws that recognized the rights and citizenship of freed black men.

The four Reconstruction Acts placed the former Confederate states under Northern military rule and then laid down the requirements the Southern states would have to meet to be readmitted to the Union. The first act created five military districts from the former Confederate states, except for previously readmitted Tennessee. The military commanders of these districts had wide-ranging powers, including the power to choose state officials. This act also required the states to ratify the Fourteenth Amendment, which had been proposed in 1866, in order to be readmitted to the Union. Three-fourths of the states must agree to an amendment for it to pass. Many Southern whites objected to obeying the Fourteenth Amendment, and the white leadership was reluctant to accept it as law.

The second Reconstruction Act took the responsibility of voter registration from Southern officials and placed it into the hands of district military leaders.

When President Johnson tried to limit the powers of these leaders, Congress gave them full authority over every aspect of voting in the third Reconstruction Act.

THE SPIRIT OF RECONSTRUCTION

After the war, social groups formed to heal the wounds of the war and slavery and bring unity to Southern communities. The Unification Movement formed in Louisiana in 1873. It was an integrated group of men from diverse races, religions, occupations, and political leanings. Their "Appeal for the Unification of the People of Louisiana" exemplified the best intentions of the spirit of Reconstruction:

Appeal for the Unification of the People of Louisiana

First—That henceforward we dedicate ourselves to the unification of our people.

Second—That by 'our people,' we mean all men, of whatever race, color or religion, who are citizens of Louisiana, and who are willing to work for her prosperity.

Third—That we shall advocate . . . the equal and impartial exercise by every citizen of Louisiana of every civil and political right guaranteed by the constitution and laws of the United States, and by the laws of honor, brotherhood, and fair dealing. . . .

Fifth—That we pledge our honor and good faith to exercise our moral influence to bring about the rapid removal of all prejudices heretofore existing against the colored citizens of Louisiana.[2]

Many white voters refused to vote on the ratification of new state constitutions, which contained laws granting freed slaves rights and civil liberties. In response, Congress passed the fourth and final Reconstruction Act on March 11, 1868, which stated that only a minority of voters was needed to ratify the state constitutions. Under these four acts, all of the former Confederate states were readmitted.

The War-Hero President

Johnson did not run for reelection in 1868. Instead, Republican general Ulysses S. Grant faced Democrat Horatio Seymour. Grant had been instrumental in winning the Civil War as the head of the Union army; Seymour was the former governor of New York. More whites voted for Seymour, but Grant carried the majority with the support of former slaves voting for the first time.

It was during the late 1860s and the 1870s that blacks enjoyed their greatest political power of the nineteenth century. Throughout the South, 1,500 blacks held various government offices. The first black US senator and US representative both took office in 1870. Grant was elected to a second term in 1872, and he

It was clear under President Grant that Northern troops were necessary to protect African Americans and their rights from white Southerners.

remained committed to improving civil rights. However, few of his policies had long-term benefits, and after he left office in 1876, the progress of Reconstruction was turned back. ∼

Chapter 4

Reconstruction Ends

Meanwhile, more than 4 million freed slaves populated the South. Most were landless and had no possessions, but they longed to realize the equality that had been promised to them. Though Southern whites feared violence, the freed people did not rise up against their former masters. They only wanted the respect and opportunity the Constitution was supposed to grant them.

White Southerners, however, saw the imposition of Northern rule and policy as yet another blow in a civil war that continued culturally. Southern whites were resentful that the wealth of the South was ruined and the workforce was in shambles. Most white Southerners held on to their previous ways of life.

The Rule of Fear and Hate

Not long after Confederate troops disbanded, groups of mostly ex-Confederate soldiers formed. These groups disrupted the political process and sought revenge for the wrongs they felt the South suffered at the hands of Northern politicians and freed blacks. A main objective of

> " The slave went free: stood a brief moment in the sun; then moved back again toward slavery."[1]
> —CIVIL RIGHTS LEADER W. E. B. DU BOIS, BLACK RECONSTRUCTION IN AMERICA, 1935

these groups was to keep blacks from voting. Of these groups, the first was perhaps the most notorious: the Ku Klux Klan.

In 1866, powerful Southern whites formed the Ku Klux Klan. By modern standards, the Klan of that era would be considered a terrorist organization. It used terror tactics to intimidate groups of people. Many white Southerners who did not participate in violent acts themselves supported the Klan's deeds by looking the

The Ku Klux Klan formed shortly after the Civil War and spread terror across the South.

other way or refusing to **testify**. Others who might have disagreed with the Klan's tactics still supported the Klan's objective of making blacks submit, and thus did nothing to oppose them. Many of those who did oppose the Klan were frightened into silence.

The head of the Klan, called the Grand Wizard, was Nathan Bedford Forrest. Forrest had been a cunning and successful Confederate cavalry commander in the war. The group dressed in white sheets and rode horses with muffled hooves so they could maintain the element of surprise. Their flowing white forms symbolized the spirits of dead Confederates coming back from the dead to avenge the South. With Forrest as their leader, the Klan terrorized blacks, immigrants, and white sympathizers across the South, beating, torturing, and even lynching anyone who opposed them. The Klan played an integral part in restoring Southern white leadership to office by intimidating black and Republican voters.

The rampant lynchings and murders became a concern to Forrest, who ordered the Ku Klux Klan disbanded in 1869. Some groups refused to disband

testify—Declare something in court under oath.

FACING VIOLENCE

In 1867, members of the black community in Calhoun, Georgia, wrote to the federal troops stationed in their area to ask for protection against the Klan. As their letter explains the situation:

> On the 16th day of the month, the Union Republican Party held a Meeting which the Colored people of the County attended en masse. Since that time we seem to have the particular hatred and spite of that class who were opposed to the principles set forth in that meeting.

> Their first act was to deprive us the privilege to worship any longer in the Church. Since we have procured one of our own, they threaten us if we hold meetings in it.

> There has been houses broken open, windows smashed and doors broken down in the dead hours of the night, men rushing in, cursing and swearing and discharging their Pistols inside the house. Men have been knocked down and unmercifully beaten and yet the authorities do not notice it at all. We would open a school here, but are almost afraid to do so, not knowing that we have any protection for life or limb.[2]

and continued their reign of terror. The situation finally drew the attention of Congress. In 1871, Congress passed three Ku Klux Klan acts, which authorized the president to use military force to quell the violence and protect blacks' voting rights. Under the acts, several thousand people were **indicted**, but Southern courts and **juries** were sympathetic to the cause of the Klan. Few of those indicted went to jail.

Louisiana had its own hate groups, one of which was the White League, formed in 1874. Like the Klan, the White League's main purpose was to interfere with a free political system by intimidating Republicans and freed blacks. In 1874, the White League killed six white men who had been given positions by a Louisiana senator from the North, along with approximately ten black witnesses. The next month, the White League occupied and took over the state government of Louisiana in New Orleans. At least 30 deaths resulted, as well as dozens of injuries.[3] In the days following the White League's surrender, not one member of the White League was **prosecuted**. Similar groups with similar purposes functioned throughout Louisiana. Plessy's act

indicted—Formally charged with an offense.

jury—A group of people selected to deliver a verdict on an issue, such as a court case.

prosecuted—Brought legal action against someone.

of defiance in 1892 was potentially life threatening—his direct challenge to the power of white supremacy could have provoked a lynching.

Racism as a Political Tool

The Southern upper class was keen to reestablish its political and economic control after the war. The South was in chaos. In addition to the millions of freed slaves, there were many poor whites. In this political turmoil, some sought to join the forces of the poor whites and the freed slaves into a single political group. The union of these two groups would be able to overwhelm the Southern upper class and stop its plans to reestablish a system of servitude in the South.

To drive a wedge between the two groups, poor whites and freed slaves, the Southern

> " Can you bear it longer, that negro [sic] ignorance, solidified in opposition to white intelligence, and led by [Northern] . . . impudence and villainy, shall continue to hold the State, your fortunes and your honor by the throat, while they perpetuate upon you indignities and crimes unparalleled?"[4]
> —A CALL FOR SUPPORTERS BY THE WHITE LEAGUE, 1870s

upper class encouraged the whites' beliefs that blacks were less than human and that association with blacks should be limited through segregation. Poor whites also saw blacks as competition for scarce jobs and land. After the end of Reconstruction, southern governments turned segregation into law, legally defining and limiting the ways blacks and whites could come together. This divide-and-conquer tactic was very successful in disempowering both poor whites and freed slaves, putting them again under the thumb of white power structures.

"The Great Betrayal"

Southern states and cities quickly began instituting laws that once again plunged blacks into servitude. During and after Reconstruction, a flurry of laws and court rulings came into effect on both sides of the issue. In 1875, the US government enacted a law in an attempt to end some types of segregation. The Civil Rights Act stated that equal accommodations for people of all colors must be provided at places such as inns and on public transportation.

With the Reconstruction Acts in place and new national and state laws that guaranteed the rights of freed slaves, it would seem there was an opportunity for the

South to revitalize itself. However, the racism and anger of white Southern officials would make this impossible. Laws previously instituted to guarantee equality would be whittled away. The South would once again institute a racist system in both law and practice. This would officially begin with the 1876 election of Republican Rutherford B. Hayes and his "Compromise of 1877," or what freed slaves called "The Great Betrayal."

Hayes's Democratic opponent was Samuel J. Tilden. In the years following the war, the Democrats had once again gained political momentum in the South. In an attempt to secure the votes of Southerners, Hayes

THE ELECTORAL COLLEGE

The US Constitution created the electoral college, although the name did not come into use until the nineteenth century. It represents a compromise between having Congress choose the president and having the people elect the president directly. Each state has a designated number of electoral college members, each of whom has one electoral vote. When citizens vote for president and vice president, they are actually voting for which candidate should win their state's electoral votes. This system means a candidate can win the most votes from citizens across the country but still lose the election if his or her opponent wins the electoral votes of enough states.

promised to withdraw Union troops from the South and return rule of the South to local governments. Despite Hayes's promises, the popular vote went to Democrat Tilden. In order to gain the one electoral vote needed to win the election, Hayes negotiated the "Compromise of 1877," which removed federal soldiers from the South, provided legislation to industrialize the South, and placed Democrats in powerful political positions in the South and among the president's advisers.

Jim Crow

In 1881, in response to the 1875 Civil Rights Act, Tennessee passed what would become the first Jim Crow law. This law stated:

> *All railroad companies located and operated in this State shall furnish separate cars, or portions of cars cut off by partition walls, in which all colored passengers who pay first class passenger rates of fare, may have the privilege to enter and occupy, and such apartments shall be kept in good repair, and with the same conveniences . . .*[5]

This was the first legal institution of a policy that would come to be known as *separate but equal.*

JIM CROW

Jim Crow was not a person but rather the name of a song sung as early as 1828. The song was typically performed by a white singer wearing blackface makeup. Ten years later, it came to be the term used to indicate separate accommodations for whites and blacks in the North and the South. There were so-called Jim Crow rail cars, for blacks only, in Massachusetts in 1841. Jim Crow eventually came to refer to a system of prejudice and segregation in which blacks were shunted off socially and legally from white society.

In 1883, the US Supreme Court ruled the Civil Rights Act of 1875 unconstitutional. This ruling instituted an era of legalized segregation and laid the ground for the *Plessy* case. Between 1887 and 1892, nine states, all Southern, enacted various Jim Crow acts regulating the creation of separate accommodations for blacks and whites in public transportation.

These Jim Crow laws came about as a direct response by whites in power to exclude an evolving black population that pushed for its rights. The 1880s saw a new generation of blacks that was less ready to defer to whites. Clashes arose between blacks who insisted upon their constitutionally guaranteed rights and whites who would deny them. Southern lawmakers used these

Segregated public areas became the norm as separate-but-equal policies spread. The label "colored" is visible above one door, *right*; the other room is for whites.

clashes to justify separate accommodations for whites and blacks, saying legislation was necessary to prevent conflict on trains.

Challenging Jim Crow

Plessy was not the first person to test train segregation policies and laws in the United States. Others risked the threat of jail, fines, or physical violence by taking a seat in the whites-only section of rail cars. Freed people and other blacks challenged the racist company policies of separating blacks and whites in rail cars by suing in court. This put railway companies' rules to the test of law. Commonly, the result was that the black person suing would lose his or her case. The decision by the court supporting a separate-but-equal policy would be established in law and create a legal **precedent**. This is what happened in the case of *West Chester and Philadelphia Railroad Company v. Miles* in 1867.

When Vera E. Miles refused to move from the whites-only section of a rail car to the colored section, little did she know that the defeat of her court case

---

precedent—A ruling that serves as an example for future rulings on similar legal cases.

would set the precedent that would legalize separate-but-equal policies across the railways of the United States. Miles had taken a seat in the whites-only section of a rail car. When the conductor asked her to move to the colored section, she refused. This led to her removal from the train. Shortly thereafter, she sued.

She won in a lower court; the judge ruled she could not be made to move due to her race. But the decision was appealed, and the case came before the Pennsylvania Supreme Court. There, the earlier ruling was reversed. Miles had lost.

Justice Daniel Agnew wrote the opinion of the court. His words would form a precedent and an excuse for segregation that would take root in the laws of other states that were hoping to keep the races separate. Agnew reasoned that women-only cars did not infringe upon the equal rights of men. So, could people be separated by other differences, such as race?

Agnew established that a railroad company had the right to separate groups that could come into conflict and that passengers had no right to object to this policy. He also said it was the carrier's responsibility to maintain the peace on its trains. Agnew asserted that God's will was to keep the races separate and that the races were

Justice Agnew's opinion helped solidify the precedent for separate-but-equal policies.

different by nature. Agnew also drew from court rulings of the 1830s, which established that the separation of blacks and whites was supported in both customs and law. Therefore, Agnew decided, as long as equal accommodations were provided, racial differences made the separation of blacks and whites "as passengers in a public conveyance the subject of a sound regulation to secure order, promote comfort, preserve the peace, and maintain the rights both of carriers and passengers."[6]

Later that same year, the Pennsylvania legislature outlawed racial discrimination on Pennsylvania railways. The next year, 1868, the Fourteenth Amendment was ratified, guaranteeing equal rights and civil liberties to all regardless of race. Even so, Agnew's decision that the separation of races was reasonable would be used by other states to justify Jim Crow policies.

Separate but equal was not the hard, fast rule. In the decade following the *Miles* decision, other people of color who had faced discrimination on the railways would **sue** in court and win. In 1873, a case brought by an African-American woman ended in a decision that opposed the separate-but-equal policy. Emma Coger was not allowed in the whites-only section of a steamship for which she had purchased a ticket. She sued and won. In the decision, the discriminatory support for separate-but-equal policies was rejected. Though the ruling found it was unlawful for race to be used as a factor in denying access to facilities on public transport, ultimately the case would hold very little national influence. ∼

sue—To bring legal action against.

Chapter 5

Fighting Segregation in New Orleans

When it came time for his act of civil disobedience in 1892, Plessy did not act alone. He was part of a coordinated movement to challenge the Separate Car Act. Plessy's arrest was orchestrated by the Citizens' Committee to Test the **Constitutionality** of the Separate Car Act. To understand Plessy and the committee, it is essential to understand the social context from which the two came; both emerged from the unique culture of the free people of color in New Orleans.

CIVIL DISOBEDIENCE

Henry David Thoreau, an American author and philosopher, coined the term *civil disobedience* in 1848. After spending a night in jail for refusing to pay a poll tax, Thoreau wrote his famous essay titled "Civil Disobedience." He wrote, "Unjust laws exist; shall we be content to obey them, or shall we endeavor to amend them . . . ?"[1] Throughout US history, ordinary individuals have engaged in civil disobedience to protest unjust laws. After the civil disobedience of Plessy and his contemporaries, their successors would use similar tactics in the twentieth century's civil rights movement.

The Free People of Color

Since its founding, New Orleans has had a rich and diverse culture. The French established New Orleans in 1718. In 1763, the Treaty of Paris transferred ownership to the Spanish. In 1800, the city was returned to France. Only three years later, France sold the Louisiana Territory, including New Orleans, to the United States. In the next decades, New Orleans would become the most important port for cotton in the United States. By 1840, the city had become the fourth-largest port in the world. French and Spanish influence, along with

constitutionality—Being in accordance with a constitution.

New Orleans woman, ca. 1880s. The people of New Orleans
had a unique culture and heritage.

the mix of people drawn to the international port city, contributed to a culture unique to New Orleans.

Free people of color, also called black creoles, were those who had white and black ancestry. Many of the free people of color came from areas of the world that had free black populations, such as Haiti or Cuba, or had bought their freedom or been freed by white owners.

The free people of color were a caste unto themselves. They were light skinned but not privileged with the full rights of whites. But unlike slaves, they did have some rights under the law. Free blacks had the right to sue and be sued and could own property. But they did not have freedom of movement. They had to get the mayor's permission to leave the city. Permission was also needed to hold gatherings or create social groups. Free blacks faced stiffer **sentences** for crimes against whites than did whites against blacks. They faced segregation in public areas, including jails, theaters, schools, and streetcars. Free blacks had to carry identification and were not allowed to be outside at night. Contact with

sentence—A decision by a judge or court including the punishment for the person convicted.

slaves was forbidden due to the fear that the two groups might organize against the whites.

Though they faced increasing racial restrictions in the first half of the nineteenth century, a great deal of social interaction still occurred between free blacks and whites in commerce and living areas. They were engineers and architects, inventors and artists. Many free blacks became excellent tradespeople, including carpenters, masons, stonecutters, and leather workers. Plessy himself was an accomplished shoemaker.

The Separate Car Act

The free people of color in New Orleans saw their place in society threatened as the liberty promised by the Reconstruction gave way to a backlash of racism.

NOT EQUAL

Though they enjoyed more freedom than pre-Civil War slaves had, the free people of color were never considered equal to whites. An 1806 Louisiana law read:

> Free people of color ought never to insult or strike white people, nor presume to conceive themselves equal to the white, but on the contrary that they ought to yield to them in every occasion, and never speak or answer to them, but with respect.[2]

Laws granting civil liberties to blacks were overturned, and in their place came laws that instituted the rule of Jim Crow. Plessy was part of the Citizens' Committee to Test the Constitutionality of the Separate Car Act, which would challenge this erosion of black rights. In particular, the committee would challenge the Separate Car Act.

Passed in July 1890, the Separate Car Act mandated that whites and blacks ride in different but equally appointed cars on all trains, excluding streetcars. Though the law gave no definition of race, it assigned conductors the duty to allot black and white passengers to their respective cars. Whites or blacks who sat in the wrong car and refused to move would be subject to a $25 fine. An exception was made for black nurses taking care of white children. Likewise, drunks and other undesirable white passengers could be moved to the black car.

As the Louisiana legislature deliberated, opposition arose among whites and blacks. One group, the American Citizens' Equal Rights Association, petitioned the legislature to strike down the bill. It asserted that citizenship is not dependent upon race, and that some arbitrary use of race should not be used to limit the rights of US citizens.

New Orleans streetcars such as this were exempted from the Separate Car Act.

Louisiana's black and some white legislators opposed the bill. Representative Victor Rochon, a black official, commented in the legislative session:

> *Why, Mr. Speaker, the idea that you and your family would not be offended in traveling hundreds of miles with a dozen or perhaps more negro servants, but [you] would be insulted to travel any distance with me and my family on account of our color.*[3]

Railroad companies also opposed the bill because it cost them money to provide additional cars. Additionally, some train company owners and workers believed the law was wrong and did not enforce it on their trains. In the end, the bill was passed and came into law. At that time, groups began planning to challenge the constitutionality of the Separate Car Act. This came in the form of the aptly

> " The law . . . which prohibits the negroes from occupying the same place in a hotel, restaurant or theatre as the whites, should prevail as to cars also. . . . Whites and blacks may there be crowded together, squeezed close to each other in the same seats, using the same conveniences. . . . The Louisiana Senate ought to step in and prevent this indignity to the white women of Louisiana."[4]
>
> —*EDITORIAL ARTICLE IN SUPPORT OF THE SEPARATE CAR ACT,* NEW ORLEANS TIMES DEMOCRAT, *JULY 9, 1890*

named Citizens' Committee to Test the Constitutionality of the Separate Car Act.

The Citizens' Committee Puts the Law to the Test

The Citizens' Committee was established on September 1, 1891. Many of its members were free people of color. Many of the older members had experienced pre–Civil War New Orleans, where the black Creoles comprised their own caste separate from the slaves. These older members knew that with the emergence of Jim Crow laws they would be subjected to the injustices the freed slaves suffered. The committee members were affluent, educated, and politically savvy. Some of

> "[The Separate Car] bill is now a law. The next thing is what are we going to do? . . . The next [thing to do] is for the American Citizens' Equal Rights Association to begin to gather funds to test the constitutionality of the law. We'll make a case, a test case, and bring it before the Federal Courts on the grounds of the invasion of the right [of] a person to travel through the States unmolested. No such case had been fairly made or presented. The American Citizens' Equal Rights Association will make it, if it understands its duty."[5]
>
> —*NEW ORLEANS* CRUSADER *EDITORIAL, JULY 19, 1890*

Middle- and upper-class blacks from around the South formed groups such as the Citizens' Committee to protect their rights.

ALBION TOURGÉE

Tourgée was a Union army veteran from Ohio. He earned his law degree after the Civil War and moved to North Carolina to fight for black rights. He became a judge, earning himself the badge of carpetbagger, an uncomplimentary term used by Southern whites to describe Northerners who came to the South after the Civil War to rebuild the region and often to make their fortunes. Eventually, he moved back North and wrote a successful novel about his experiences in the South, *A Fool's Errand: By One of the Fools*.

the members were so light skinned that, had they wished, they could have easily abandoned the cause and blended into white society. Younger members such as newspaper owner Louis Andre Martinet had come of age during Reconstruction.

Martinet used his paper, the *Crusader*, to urge readers to oppose the Separate Car Act, calling for a **test case** to challenge the constitutionality of the law. Martinet secured the services of Albion Tourgée, a white New York lawyer who had championed the movement for black rights. Tourgée became the committee's lead

test case—A case that is likely to set a precedent for future rulings.

counselor. He consulted with a local lawyer, who would try any resulting cases in Louisiana. The committee raised funds, and with its new legal team it began mapping out a strategy to defeat the law.

The committee's first attempt to bring down the Separate Car Act began on February 24, 1892. A son of a committee member, Daniel Desdunes, was provided with a first-class ticket for a trip from New Orleans to Mobile, Alabama. The ticket was for a whites-only car of the train. Desdunes, who was extremely fair skinned and could have passed for white, took his seat without notice, and the train departed.

The event had been coordinated with the train company. Before the train left New Orleans city limits, the conductor asked Desdunes to move to the Jim Crow car as planned. Detectives hired by the committee then arrested Desdunes for violating the Separate Car Act. Desdunes was taken to jail, but the committee soon bailed him out.

Unfortunately, the *Desdunes* case would not be the test case the committee had hoped for. Desdunes's ticket had been for an interstate trip. Before the *Desdunes* case was tried, a similar case appeared before the Louisiana state court. In that case, the court ruled that the federal

Tourgée worked with the Citizens' Committee from his New York home.

government, not the state of Louisiana, regulated interstate commerce. Therefore, the Separate Car Act did not apply to trains crossing state lines. The charges against Desdunes were dismissed since he had not broken the Separate Car Act after all. With no broken law, there was no case, and the committee was back to the beginning.

Shortly after the dismissal of the *Desdunes* case, the committee chose Plessy to lead another action to challenge the Separate Car Act. This time, the ticket would be for intrastate travel; the trip would take place entirely within the state of Louisiana. What would follow would strike at the heart of the Separate Car Act and test the US Constitution itself.

Plessy Steps Aboard

Plessy took his short yet historic ride in an ambiguous political climate. Blacks had been guaranteed the rights and freedoms of whites by the Thirteenth, Fourteenth, and Fifteenth amendments, and some, such as Coger, had brought suits to challenge racist transportation laws and had won. Even so, laws such as Louisiana's Separate Car Act were being instituted as Southern Democrats energetically resumed the reins of political power in the

JAMES WALKER

In his mid-fifties, Walker was experienced and known as a "good, upright, and conscientious man."[6] Walker had fought in the Civil War for the Confederacy, serving from 1862 to 1865. After the war, Walker moved to the Republican side and was active in local politics. He eventually quit politics in disgust over the dealings of some members of his party and focused instead on his legal practice. Walker did not take the case for free, but he charged less than half as much as another attorney who was considered for the position.

South. Although the Citizens' Committee did not get the test case they planned with Desdunes, the dismissal of the case struck a blow against Jim Crow laws for interstate travel. Now, it was time for the Citizens' Committee to challenge the constitutionality of the Separate Car Act in respect to intrastate travel.

After the dismissal of the *Desdunes* case, the Citizens' Committee, with Martinet leading the way, coordinated another act of disobedience designed to challenge Louisiana's Separate Car Act. Tourgée was again at the helm of the Citizens' Committee legal team. He coordinated the defense from New York. Joining him was local attorney James Walker, who had acted as the *Desdunes* attorney in New Orleans. Though correspondence was slow due to the mail system,

Tourgée and Walker were able to agree upon a strategy. On June 7, 1892, Plessy refused to leave the whites-only section of the train, and with Plessy's arrest, the plan was set into motion. ∼

Chapter 6

The *Plessy* Case Begins

O n October 28, 1892, hearings for the case of *Homer Plessy v. The State of Louisiana* began before Judge John Howard Ferguson in the state criminal district court. Ferguson had only been serving on the bench in New Orleans for four months when the *Plessy* case came before him. Ferguson was originally from Massachusetts, where he had studied law under lawyer and abolitionist Benjamin Hallett. A Northern Democrat, Hallett had staunchly opposed slavery of any kind prior to the Civil War.

The defense did not expect to win in the local court; it also expected to lose any appeal to the

Louisiana Supreme Court. Rather, the defense aimed
to take the case to the US Supreme Court in order to
challenge segregation across the entire country.

The First Hearing

Lawyers for both sides had previously submitted written
briefs to Judge Ferguson. Now they would make **oral
arguments**, and Ferguson would decide if the case
should go to trial or if it should be dismissed.

Defense attorney Walker argued that Plessy's
arrest violated his **constitutional** rights, specifically his
Thirteenth and Fourteenth amendment rights. Walker
asserted that forcing Plessy from the whites-only car
merely due to his race was equivalent to placing upon
him one of the "badges of slavery" that was expressly
forbidden by the Thirteenth Amendment. In other
words, due to his race, Plessy was being treated as an
inferior just as slaves had been. Also, Walker argued,
the Fourteenth Amendment guaranteed Plessy the same
civil liberties and rights under the law as any other US

brief—A document that establishes the legal argument of a case.
constitutional—In accordance with a constitution.
oral argument—A spoken presentation of a legal case by a lawyer.

citizen. In addition, the Fourteenth Amendment forbade states from limiting the rights of US citizens. Walker said the Separate Car Act did just that. Walker argued the law was so flawed that the case should not even go to court. However, if Ferguson ruled the case should go to trial, Walker could appeal that decision to the Louisiana Supreme Court, rather than waiting for a ruling on the case itself.

Assistant district attorney Lionel Adams presented the case for the state. Attorney Adams was experienced as both a **prosecutor** and defense attorney. Adams cited the Separate Car Act and the fact that **testimony** showed Plessy deliberately broke the law. Adams asserted the Separate Car Act was fair because it was just as illegal for whites to occupy the Jim Crow cars as it was for blacks to sit in the whites-only cars. The purpose of the law, he argued, was to prevent the conflict that could arise should the two races share cars. Whites also, according to Adams, had the right to ride without being exposed to the "foul odors" of black riders.[1] Adams cited other

prosecutor—A lawyer who brings legal action against someone.
testimony—Something declared in court under oath.

LIONEL ADAMS

Lionel Adams was considered one of the best trial lawyers of his day. Just a year before the *Plessy* trial began, Adams had represented a group of Italians, a minority in New Orleans, who were accused of assassinating New Orleans police chief David Hennessy in 1891. Adams had been the chief prosecutor but had taken the assistant district attorney position so his peer, Charles Butler, could gain experience in the role of district attorney.

Adams's past was not without controversy, however. A citizens' group investigating the Hennessy assassination trial accused the Adams team of tampering with the jury. They claimed Adams arranged to have the lights dimmed when the jury visited the Hennessy murder scene. Ultimately, no formal charges were made, and Adams continued to serve the New Orleans court.

federal cases that supported the constitutionality of the Separate Car Act.

On November 18, 1892, Ferguson gave his decision. He complimented the defense on its arguments, but sided with the state of Louisiana. The charges would stand and Plessy's trial would move forward. Ferguson made his ruling because the majority of previous cases supported Adams's argument that the state had a right to keep the peace by separating the races on railway cars. In his decision, Ferguson did not address the defense's assertion that Plessy's Thirteenth and Fourteenth amendment rights were violated. Plessy's lawyers made ready to appeal Ferguson's decision to the Louisiana Supreme Court. This action would delay Plessy's criminal trial.

Less than one week after Judge Ferguson handed down his decision, Walker began the process of appealing to the state supreme court. Tourgée would join him in person to argue in front of the high court. There was little chance of winning the case at the state level. State judges could be influenced by the political leanings of their constituents and the state legislature. Their careers depended on the support of the legislature, and in this case the legislature was intent on legalizing Jim Crow in transportation as well as other areas of life. Defeat at the state level was in fact part of the team's plan because it would allow for an appeal to the US Supreme Court.

The Louisiana Supreme Court

When it reached the Louisiana Supreme Court, the *Plessy* case became known as *Ex Parte Plessy*, or "in the interest of Plessy." Before the court, Tourgée and Walker used three basic premises to argue the unconstitutionality of the Separate Car Act. The law, they said first, was not clear in its language and meaning. Second, it put train conductors in the unfair position of determining the race of passengers. And third, the law violated the US Constitution, and in particular the Thirteenth and Fourteenth amendments.

Tourgée and Walker argued the language of the Separate Car Act lacked clarity. The law referred to "persons of the colored race" but provided no real criteria for determining what constituted the colored race.[2] This left the decision up to the conductor whether a person was to be considered colored or white. Tourgée and Walker provided 16 different legal definitions of Negro or mulatto.

> The trouble with [the Separate Car] law is that it perpetuates race prejudice among citizens of the United States, and that the spirit of cast[e] and race is exemplified in the spirit of legislation."[3]
>
> —*FROM TOURGÉE AND WALKER'S BRIEF PREPARED FOR THE LOUISIANA SUPREME COURT*

Light-skinned blacks ran the risk of losing their seat or their ticket if they chose the wrong area in which to sit. The distinction of race would be much more evident with dark-skinned blacks, who would be confined to

Although it was illegal for African Americans to be passengers in whites-only cars, African Americans worked in such cars as waiters and other servants.

the Jim Crow cars. They argued this was a violation of the Fourteenth Amendment, which promised equal protection under the law regardless of race.

In addition, Tourgée and Walker found it hard to justify the allowance for black nurses or nannies to be allowed in the whites-only cars. They noted the law purported to prevent contact between the races, but they argued the law's true purpose was to prevent contact as equals, since black nurses and servants were allowed contact with whites in the whites-only cars. To them, this was absurd—a white man's black nanny would be allowed in the whites-only car, but the black wife of the same white man would not. The nanny, therefore, would be privileged to rights the wife herself was not allowed.

Tourgée and Walker also found it contradictory that the law applied only to railway trains. Presumably, the law was put into effect to minimize tensions between races. Walker and Tourgée wondered why the law did not apply to streetcars where "contact between white and colored persons . . . is more immediate, and many thousand times more frequent."[4] Another discrepancy in the Separate Car Act, according to Tourgée and Walker, was that in deciding the race of a passenger, train conductors were basically becoming agents of the court. This put citizens at risk because if they were put off a train by a conductor due to his assignment of race, they were in effect being prosecuted without due process of law.

Tourgée and Walker also asserted that the Separate Car Act directly violated the Thirteenth and Fourteenth amendments. They repeated Walker's arguments from district court that the Separate Car Act had made being black a "badge of servitude." They also argued that Plessy's Fourteenth Amendment rights were being violated. Tourgée and Walker claimed the Separate Car Act "abridge[d] the rights, privileges, and immunities of citizens on account of race and color."[6]

> " What else but a badge of servitude is imposed and perpetuated . . . when a person, seven-eighths white and one-eighth of colored blood, or a person fifteen-sixteenths parts white and one-sixteenth part of colored blood, is subjected to fine or imprisonment by authority of State law, for insisting (contrary to a conductor's judgment) that he or she, as the case may be, should be classed as a white person . . . ?"[5]
>
> — *FROM TOURGÉE AND WALKER'S BRIEF PREPARED FOR THE LOUISIANA SUPREME COURT*

The State's Arguments

Arguing the case for the state again was Adams. Adams saw nothing unconstitutional with the Separate Car Act and, like Judge Ferguson, believed the trial should proceed.

Adams argued that it was up to the state to decide what happened on the state railways. The Thirteenth and Fourteenth amendments, according to Adams, guaranteed political rights, such as the right to vote, but did not dictate social rights, such as which groups could or could not mingle. Also, Adams said the restrictions on the two races were equal, since the penalty for a white person sitting in a Jim Crow car was the same as for a black person sitting in a whites-only car. He then cited a number of cases that supported his position, including an 1885 Tennessee case where the judge ruled, "Equal accommodations do not mean identical accommodations."[7] Adams asserted that all travel had its discomforts and that all travelers had to be flexible about these—though in truth, the accommodations in the Jim Crow cars were far worse than those of the whites-only cars.

The Decision

On December 19, 1892, the Louisiana Supreme Court announced its decision. The verdict was unanimously against Plessy. Justice Charles E. Fenner handed down the court's opinion.

Fenner cited a number of previous cases to support the court's decision. He found that the US Supreme Court had not ruled one way or the other on the legality of segregating rail cars as long as the accommodations were equal. He gave as evidence 16 state and lower federal court decisions that resulted in **statutes** or regulations enforcing the separations of the races as long as the "facilities or accommodations provided are substantially equal."[8]

As to the idea that segregation contributed to race prejudice, Fenner cited a decision from a Massachusetts Supreme Court ruling in which a justice had implied such prejudices were not created by laws and could not be changed legally. Fenner asserted that the mixing of the races could lead to increased prejudices and that keeping the races apart would lessen them. Fenner did

statute—A law put into effect by the legislative branch of government.

In the 1890s, the Louisiana Supreme Court met in the Cabildo. Today, the building is a museum.

not acknowledge the fact that this ruling, which justified segregating Massachusetts schools, was followed six years later by a law ending school segregation.

Another case Fenner cited implied that some of the differences between whites and blacks were from God. In this Pennsylvania ruling, which Fenner quoted, Justice Agnew stated that "to assert separateness is not to declare inferiority in either. It is simply to say that, following

> Yesterday the Supreme Court of Louisiana rendered a decision in favor of the constitutionality of the Separate Car Act on practically the same grounds as led Judge Ferguson, of the Criminal Court, to, the same conclusion. . . .
>
> "The community at large will be glad to hear that this race question is settled by the supreme tribunal of the state; and that it is settled on grounds which must commend themselves to the enlightened sentiment as well of the colored as of the white citizens. The two races will not mix, any more than oil and water; and it is better that the fact should be recognized at once, and made binding on both races by a law which will render all deliberate attempts at mixing penal."[11]
>
> —NEW ORLEANS TIMES-DEMOCRAT, *DECEMBER 20, 1892*

the orders of Divine Providence, human authority ought not to compel these widely-separated races to intermix."[9] Agnew also said the differences between whites and blacks were so significant that their separation on public transportation was "the subject of a sound regulation to secure order, promote comfort, preserve the peace, and maintain the rights both of carriers and passengers."[10] Both the Massachusetts and the Pennsylvania cases Fenner cited were decided before the ratification of the Fourteenth Amendment.

Ultimately, Fenner found the Separate Car Act was valid because segregation on public transport was "in the interest of public order, peace and comfort."[12] The law, he said, applied to both races equally, since the penalties for both whites and black were the same should either violate the law. The Separate Car Act would stand.

So, as the Tourgée-Walker team predicted, the case was not dismissed in the Louisiana Supreme Court. This was not bad news, however. The Citizens' Committee had always wanted to test the constitutionality of the Separate Car Act in the highest court of the land. A win there would set a precedent that could make Jim Crow illegal throughout the country. ∼

Chapter 7

A Changing Society

*I*n 1893, as the *Plessy* case worked its way to the US Supreme Court, a period of economic prosperity ended with the Panic of 1893. The economic depression that followed would last for five years, becoming one of the worst in US history. The impact of this depression was far-reaching, and it hindered efforts to forward the rights of black Americans. More than 15,000 businesses and 642 banks failed, and 20 percent of the US workforce, between 2 and 3 million people, lost jobs.[1]

The depression hit when unions were beginning to organize to secure the rights of black and white workers. With the onset of the depression in 1893,

The 1893 depression worsened conditions for many poor black Americans.

however, employers sought to dismantle the unions. They began hiring black workers for a lower hourly wage than white workers. They also brought in black workers to replace striking whites. This caused racial friction.

Across the country, a small group of rich and powerful white men amassed more and more of the country's wealth. Their wealth allowed them great political influence, which caused policies in Congress and the Supreme Court to become increasingly friendly to business and increasingly in favor of states' rights instead of federal government oversight.

This shift in the political tenor brought the Fourteenth Amendment under new examination. The business-friendly climate brought the US Supreme Court to a new interpretation of the amendment. Many of the justices were former corporate lawyers, and they were more focused on problems faced by corporations than those faced by African Americans. The justices came to believe that, rather than protecting the civil rights of freedmen and other blacks, the Fourteenth Amendment was meant to protect the rights of corporations. Their logic was that corporations were legally "persons," so states could not take corporate property without "due process of law" as called for in the amendment.

This drastically weakened the original intent of the amendment.

WHITE AND BLACK UNIONS

The American Federation of Labor (AFL) union organized whites and blacks together. Established in 1881, the AFL initially encouraged the integration of its local unions, or at least a separate-but-equal policy. By uniting the workforce, the AFL's ranks would grow, and increased membership would increase its bargaining power. In 1882, the AFL denied membership to two organizations because they included whites-only clauses in their constitutions.

When the 1893 depression hit, however, the AFL abandoned its policy of integration. By the end of the depression, the AFL supported segregation and even blamed blacks for racial tensions in the organization.

During the same period, a political group called the Populists sought to join white and black farm workers into one political group. The Populists also hoped to increase their political power by combining black and white workers. The Populists focused on the shared economic challenges faced by both blacks and whites. But the white Democrats in power in the South had little interest in securing the rights of black farmers. Elections were rife with fraud and intimidation. The chances of the interracial agrarian movement of the Populists in the South were crushed. The movement became infected with racism, and many blacks returned to the Republican Party.

Meanwhile, the Plessy team prepared its appeal to the US Supreme Court. The case would be known as *Plessy v. Ferguson* because Plessy was challenging decisions made in the hearing before Judge Ferguson, not the outcome of his criminal trial, which had not yet occurred. The team had to file a petition for a **writ of certiorari** asking the court to hear the case. The court had a large backload of cases, so it could be years before the case was heard, if the court agreed to hear it at all. The team also had to file for a writ of prohibition to stop Plessy's criminal trial until the Supreme Court case was resolved. It also prepared briefs, outlining the arguments it would make before the court. Plessy's attorneys finished filing their paperwork in February 1893, and the court agreed to hear the case. Initially, Tourgée considered asking the court to put the case on a fast track. However, Tourgée reconsidered, realizing the sitting justices were not likely to rule in his favor. He hoped the makeup of the court would change in the time it took their case to move forward. In the

writ of certiorari—An order from a higher court to a lower court calling for the record of a case for review.

meantime, the racist policies that had begun with the end of Reconstruction continued to take hold and grow.

Martinet Questions the Movement

Later in 1893, after the Louisiana Supreme Court had ruled, Martinet spent time as a medical student in Chicago, Illinois. There he met black businessmen who were able to establish their own businesses and property. This made him reflect on the disempowerment that Southern blacks experienced back home in Louisiana. He began to dread returning to the South and even began to doubt the effectiveness of the struggle for racial equality.

In a letter to Tourgée, Martinet wondered if the struggle was helping or hurting blacks. He wrote that it seemed like when blacks showed "any spirit—manifest any appreciation of the labors and sacrifices on their behalf . . . 'white supremacy' is sure to assert itself, rise up and crush it."[2]

In fact, Martinet's writings revealed his fear that any attempt to assert black rights would actually bring more oppression from whites. Though his paper, the *Crusader*, had stated that submission to oppression only strengthened the oppressor, Martinet wondered if the opposite was true:

> *Are we not fighting a hopeless battle . . . a battle made doubly hopeless by the tyranny and cruelty of the Southern white? Are the Negroes progressing, or are they not retrograding under the yoke of the Southern [white] barbarians, and are not our efforts for their betterment put forth in a method & manner calculated to do little good, or perhaps harm?*[3]

EXPERIENCING RACISM

Martinet experienced the relative freedoms of blacks in the Northern states and contrasted life in the North to life in the Jim Crow South. In a May 1893 letter to Tourgée, he writes about what it means to experience racism:

> *You don't know what that feeling is, [Tourgée]. You may imagine it, but you have never experienced it. Knowing that you are a freeman, & yet not allowed to enjoy a freeman's liberty, rights, and privileges unless you stake your life every time you try it. To live always under the feeling of restraint is worse than living behind prison bars. My heart is constricted at the very thought of returning [to the South]—it suffocates me.*[4]

Ultimately, Martinet realized that for any gains to be made, blacks had to be educated and fight for their rights. But he wondered just how this could happen in the Jim Crow South.

The Citizens' Committee Continues the Fight

While waiting for the *Plessy* case to move to the Supreme Court, the Citizens' Committee was not idle. Martinet returned to Louisiana and with the help of the Citizens' Committee turned the *Crusader* into a daily paper, the only black daily newspaper in the United States. To make this possible, printers and laborers worked for half their usual wage and editors worked for free. The paper became the voice of the Citizens' Committee and continued to speak out against racial injustices. Writers challenged segregation in trains and churches and called attention to the injustice of all-white juries and attempted bans on interracial marriages.

The *Crusader* continued reporting on race issues as the laws of Louisiana became increasingly restrictive. In 1894, the Louisiana legislature banned all interracial marriages and forbade any such marriages to be performed. This was a return to pre-Reconstruction policies; interracial marriage had only been legal in the state since 1870. Also, the Louisiana legislature amended the Separate Car Act to require segregated waiting rooms as well as segregated rail cars.

The Citizens' Committee fought for equal rights against racism. The movement celebrated the rights

FACING VIOLENCE

Black people who stood up for their constitutionally guaranteed rights often faced ridicule, intimidation, or violence at the hands of white citizens, including the military and officers of the law. S. R. Kendrick wrote a letter in July 1892 in support of Tourgée's work for civil rights. Kendrick explains circumstances in the South:

> Surely you do not realize the situation as we do, who lives here, the man or Woman who attempts to strike a Blow here for Freedom [will] be killed out right— or he [will] be Exiled from all he possesses. . . . We are a little tired of having to show our Corpse to prove to the world that the Laws of this Country is not sufficient to protect the Black man as well as the white. . . . In a word we see no possible chance of ever being Free under The Flag of Liberty and Christian civilization. . . . There are standing armies in every county in every Southern State . . . who are Negro haters and who are willing to sacrifice everything even Life in order to give the negro to know that he must obey the white man.[5]

and humanity of all, not one group over another. The committee did not want to pit blacks against whites. When the Catholic Church opened a separate black church, the *Crusader* responded:

> *Separation in one form may bring separation in another. . . . The colored people were created by the same God who created other nations of men, and like others, they were born to live in society with their neighbors so as to contribute their share of responsibility on this planet. . . . If men are divided by, or in, the Church, where can they be united in the bonds of faith and love of truth and justice?*[6]

Booker T. Washington and the Philosophy of Accommodation

While the Plessy team waited for the case to appear before the Supreme Court, the equal rights movement lost two powerful activists. One was Aristide Mary of New Orleans. Mary's father was white and his mother was black. He had been a powerful leader for equal rights before the Civil War and afterward. He was a cofounder of the multiracial, multiethnic Unification Movement in 1873. It was at his request the Citizens'

Committee was born. His death was a great blow to the movement.

Another powerful figure who died during this time was Frederick Douglass. An escaped slave and son of a white man and his black female slave, Douglass was one of the leading abolitionists of his time. He spent his adult life speaking out against slavery and, after the war, he campaigned for equal rights. He was an influential political figure and consistent voice for the disenfranchised, including blacks and women. He died in 1895.

After the deaths of these two influential proponents of equal rights, another figure sought to step into the void left by Mary and Douglass. This was the African-American leader Booker T. Washington. Instead of fighting for equal rights, Washington pushed a platform of accommodation and separation, rejecting militancy. He advocated for education so blacks could improve their economic situations. This won him favor with Northern industrialists and Southern separatists. Washington's approach did not directly oppose the white power structure by demanding equal rights.

In his famous speech, later called the Atlanta compromise, Washington conceded the subordinate

Booker T. Washington emerged in the 1890s as one of the country's most important African-American leaders.

CALLING FOR COMPROMISE

While the Citizens' Committee continued fighting for equality, influential black leader Booker T. Washington pushed for compromise, writing in September 1895:

> *In all things that are purely social, we can be as separate as the fingers, yet one as the hand in all things essential to mutual progress. . . . The wisest among my race understand that the agitation of questions of social equality is the extremest folly, and that progress in the enjoyment of all the privileges that will come to us must be the result of severe and constant struggle rather than of artificial forcing. . . . The opportunity to earn a dollar in a factory just now is worth infinitely more than the opportunity to spend a dollar in an opera-house.*[7]

position of the blacks in post-Reconstruction America. Washington felt blacks needed opportunities to participate in economic matters in the South, but he thought they should give up on reaching political and social equality with whites. In his speech, Washington said blacks and whites could be separate in the social realm, but in industry the two could work together.

It was in this social and political climate that the *Plessy* case progressed toward the Supreme Court. The rights of blacks were being degraded throughout the country, either through legal channels or through intimidation, and segregation was becoming more prevalent. In April 1896, the Supreme Court would hear the *Plessy* case. Its ruling would decide the fate of the millions of blacks who lived at the mercy of Jim Crow. ～

Chapter 8

The Supreme Court

As the *Plessy* case waited its turn to go before the US Supreme Court, Tourgée saw a glimmer of hope that the court might return a favorable verdict. He knew only one of the justices was likely to rule in Plessy's favor. But he had a plan for the others. He believed if the Citizens' Committee could get the case national attention, he could sway the votes of other justices.

The Supreme Court Tourgée faced had become overwhelmingly pro-business and anti-civil rights. The justices of the court were all white and affluent. Two justices were from former Confederate states, Tennessee and Louisiana. A third was from border

PLESSY'S SUPREME COURT

Melville W. Fuller served as chief justice when the *Plessy* case arrived in the Supreme Court. Fuller was a Northerner who had helped Democrat Stephen Douglas run for president against Lincoln in 1860. He was known to be sympathetic to large corporations. Under Fuller, the other justices who heard the *Plessy* case were: David J. Brewer, Henry B. Brown, Stephen J. Field, Horace Gray, John M. Harlan, Howell E. Jackson, George Shiras Jr., and Edward D. White.

state Kentucky, which had permitted slavery but did not secede during the Civil War; the rest were from the North. All were appointed in the years following Reconstruction except for Justice Stephen J. Field, who was appointed by President Lincoln in 1863.

The one clear voice of disagreement on the court was Justice John Marshall Harlan of Kentucky. Harlan had served in the Union army during the war, though he did not believe in the abolition of slavery. He felt abolition would interfere with property rights. However, he had a half brother who was black, and he became a voice on the court supporting equal rights.

The Citizens' Committee worked to advance the cause in the years between the hearings. Unfortunately for

The Plessy team hoped Justice Harlan would support their cause.

Plessy and Tourgée, however, when the case came before the Supreme Court in 1896, there was little evidence that any kind of public outcry was raised to sway the judges.

The Trial Begins

On April 13, 1896, Tourgée presented the *Plessy* case to the Supreme Court. Helping him was an old friend, attorney Samuel F. Philips, who had unsuccessfully argued an earlier civil rights case before the Supreme Court.

Tourgée hoped to appeal to the pro-business leanings of the court. He pointed out that forcing train companies to provide separate cars for blacks imposed undue expenses. He argued that the state of Louisiana did not have the right to interfere with business in this way. The court also highly prized property rights, so Tourgée presented Plessy's right to ride as a form of property.

Tourgée's main point was that the Separate Car Act was unconstitutional because it violated the terms of national citizenship guaranteed by the Fourteenth Amendment. Tourgée argued that the rights of national citizenship should not be hindered by state citizenship:

The old citizenship of the United States was determined by race or descent. The new citizenship of the United States had nothing to do with race or descent. Under the pre-existing law no man having a drop of colored blood in his veins, could become a citizen of the United States. It was in all literalness a "white man's government." In the new citizenship color is expressly ignored and the sole condition of citizenship, is birth in the United

States. . . . [The Separate Car Act's] only effect is to perpetuate the stigma of color—to make the curse immortal, incurable, inevitable.[1]

The attorney for the state of Louisiana, Milton J. Cunningham, relied strictly on the Louisiana Supreme Court ruling. He cited a previous US Supreme Court ruling in the *Civil Rights Cases* in which Justice Joseph Bradley had found that refusing public accommodations on the basis of race did not violate the Thirteenth Amendment. Cunningham said in this particular case, Plessy had not shown that the Jim Crow car accommodations were inferior to the white ones, and thus he had not been discriminated against due to his color. In this case, Cunningham added, equal accommodations did not mean identical accommodations. The two needed only be approximately equal.

The Supreme Court Decides

On May 18, 1896, the Supreme Court ruled on the *Plessy* case. It was almost four years after Plessy had told the train conductor he was a "colored man." In these years, Plessy and the members of the Citizens' Committee who had arranged for the test case had

CITING PRECEDENT

In the majority opinion, Justice Brown cited the court's ruling that struck down the Civil Rights Act in 1883. Brown agreed with the earlier court that the Thirteenth Amendment could not be used to prevent discrimination. In the earlier ruling, Justice Bradley had stated:

> *It would be running the slavery argument into the ground to make it apply to every act of discrimination which a person may see fit to make as to the guests he will entertain, or as to the people he will take into his coach or cab or car, or admit to his concert or theatre, or deal with in other matters of intercourse or business.*[2]

worked to appeal the *Plessy* case to the highest court in the land. In this they were successful. But when the ruling came down, their hopes of defeating Jim Crow were dashed. The court found the Separate Car Act was constitutional in a vote of seven to one. Justice David J. Brewer did not vote because his daughter had died and he left Washington DC during the arguments.

Justice Henry B. Brown wrote the **majority opinion**. Brown found Plessy's Thirteenth Amendment

majority opinion—An explanation of the reasoning behind the majority decision of the Supreme Court.

Supreme Court of the United States,

No. 210 , October Term, 1895.

Homer Adolph Plessy
Plaintiff in Error,

vs.

J. H. Ferguson, Judge of Section "A" Criminal District Court for the Parish of Orleans.

In Error to the *Supreme* Court of the State of *Louisiana*

This cause came on to be heard on the transcript of the record from the *Supreme* Court of the State of *Louisiana* and was argued by counsel.

On consideration whereof, It is now here ordered and adjudged by this Court that the judgment of the said *Supreme* Court, in this cause, be, and the same is hereby, *Affirmed with Costs.*

Per Mr. Justice Brown
May 18, 1896.

Dissenting:

Mr Justice Harlan

The Supreme Court ruling in *Plessy v. Ferguson*

rights had not been violated. The Separate Car Act did not enslave Plessy. Brown relied upon the court's previous ruling in the *Civil Rights Cases*, which found that merely making a distinction by race did not "destroy the legal equality of the two races, or reestablish a state of involuntary servitude."[3]

Brown also found Plessy's Fourteenth Amendment rights had not been violated. The Fourteenth Amendment guaranteed political rights, but when it came to social rights, the states had jurisdiction. As long as it was for the public good, explained Brown, states could require the separation of blacks and whites.

Brown concluded that social equality could not be legislated. He wrote that the mere separation of the races did not imply the inferiority of blacks, and that if blacks felt inferior, it was something they were putting upon themselves:

> If the two races are to meet upon terms of social equality, it must be the result of natural affinities, a mutual appreciation of each other's merits, and a voluntary consent of individuals. . . . Legislation is powerless to eradicate racial instincts or to abolish distinctions based upon physical differences, and the attempt to do so can only result in accentuating the

difficulties of the present situation. If the civil and political rights of both races be equal, one cannot be inferior to the other civilly or politically. If one race be inferior to the other socially, the Constitution of the United States cannot put them upon the same plane.[4]

> We consider the underlying fallacy of the plaintiff's argument to consist in the assumption that the enforced separation of the two races stamps the colored race with a badge of inferiority. If this be so, it is not by reason of anything found in the act, but solely because the colored race chooses to put that construction upon it. . . . The argument also assumes that social prejudices may be overcome by legislation, and that equal rights cannot be secured to the negro except by an enforced commingling of the two races. We cannot accept this proposition."[5]
> —*JUSTICE BROWN'S MAJORITY OPINION*

The one dissenting voice was Justice Harlan. In his **dissent**, Harlan wrote that the idea of distinguishing between races in the law was against the Constitution. He saw that the decision in the *Plessy* case would "in time, prove to be quite as

dissent—An official written statement of a Supreme Court justice who disagrees with the majority decision.

110

pernicious as the decision made by [the Supreme Court] in the Dred Scott Case."[6] He believed legislation such as the Separate Car Act was not intended to help keep the peace, but instead it was intended to promote conflict between blacks and whites. None, he said, were served in such a system. Personal liberty could not exist in a state that legislated segregation.

Back to Judge Ferguson's Court

On January 11, 1897, Plessy appeared in court in New Orleans before Judge Ferguson. He withdrew his plea of not guilty and entered a plea of guilty. He was fined $25, which he paid.

> "But in view of the Constitution, in the eye of the law, there is in this country no superior, dominant, ruling class of citizens. There is no caste here. Our Constitution is color-blind, and neither knows nor tolerates classes among citizens. In respect of civil rights, all citizens are equal before the law. . . . It is, therefore, to be regretted that this high tribunal . . . has reached the conclusion that it is competent for a state to regulate the enjoyment by citizens of their civil rights solely upon the basis of race."[8]
>
> —*JUSTICE HARLAN'S DISSENT*

Plessy and the Citizens' Committee had been defeated. The highest court in the land had found the Separate Car Act constitutional. Segregation was legal. The result would be decades of discrimination at the hands of Jim Crow. ~

T. & P. RY. TRAIN BULLETIN, DAT

EASTWARD			WESTWARD	
TRAIN	TIME DUE	WILL ARRIVE	TRAIN	TIME DUE
94	3 PM		95	11 AM

REMARKS

No 94 Runs Mondays Wednesdays & Fri
No 95 Do Tuesday Thursdays & Sat

ORED

Trains and train stations remained segregated after the
Plessy ruling.

Chapter 9

After *Plessy*

*A*fter the Supreme Court decision, the Citizens' Committee disbanded. Its purpose had been fulfilled, though the outcome was not what the members had hoped for. In their last statement they said:

> Notwithstanding this decision . . . we, as freemen, still believe that we were right and our cause is sacred. We are encouraged by the indomitable will and noble defense of Hon. Albion W. Tourgée, and supported by the courageous dissenting opinion of Justice John Harlan in behalf of justice and equal rights. In defending the cause of liberty, we met with defeat, but not with ignominy.[1]

The *Plessy* ruling solidified separate-but-equal policies in US law.

After settling accounts and distributing some money to charities, the defense committee sent Tourgée six dollars. Tourgée had agreed to work the case for free. Plessy returned to his craft as a shoemaker. He lived the rest of his life in New Orleans and died on March 1, 1925.

The *Plessy* ruling opened the door for a flood of new Jim Crow laws throughout the South. Laws segregated water fountains, bathrooms, and phone booths. Separate hospitals served black and white patients. There were separate cemeteries as well. Public schools were segregated. One Alabama law made it illegal for whites and blacks to play a game of checkers together. Although Congress had forbidden Jim Crow cars for interstate rail travel, in 1898, a Tennessee court ruled that interstate trains could be forcibly segregated. Many Northern states enacted separate-but-equal laws as well.

Taking Away the Vote

In 1898, Louisiana held a constitutional convention to revise the Louisiana Constitution. The convention's intent was to disenfranchise as many blacks as possible. The convention adopted several different provisions for voting, so that if a black voter could meet one of the provisions, he might be disqualified under another.

While the language of the Separate Car Act had provided for separate accommodations that were at least equal on paper, that kind of language was absent in the constitutional convention. Members were unashamedly focused on removing blacks from voting rolls. The chairman of the Judiciary Committee, Thomas Semmes, announced:

We met here to establish the supremacy of the white race and the white race constitutes the Democratic Party of this State. Our mission was to establish the supremacy of the white race in this state to the extent to which it could be legally and constitutionally done . . . We have established throughout the State white manhood suffrage.[2]

The result of these white legislators' efforts was the so-called grandfather clause. Since there were provisions that required literacy or the ownership of property in order to vote, many illiterate and poor whites would be excluded from voting. The grandfather clause made it possible for these whites to qualify for the vote. The clause provided that men who were eligible

> " No male person who was on January 1st, 1867, or at any date prior thereto, entitled to vote under the Constitution or statutes of any State of the United States, wherein he then resided, and no son or grandson of any such person . . . shall be denied the right to register and vote in this State by reason of his failure to possess the educational or property qualifications prescribed by this Constitution."[3]
>
> —*THE GRANDFATHER CLAUSE, 1898, LOUISIANA STATE CONSTITUTION*

to vote before or on January 1, 1867, could not be denied the right to register to vote. In addition, the son and grandson of such a person would have the right to register to vote. These rights applied even if the person met no other requirements for voting. In other words, the grandfather clause provided the vote to illiterate and poor whites. But it did not apply to blacks, since blacks did not have the right to vote on or before January 1, 1867.

The clause served its purpose. In 1897, black voters comprised 44 percent of voters. By 1900, less than four percent of eligible voters were black. In those three years, more than 120,000 blacks had been removed from voter rolls.[4]

Fighting Back

Although separate but equal was the law of the land, courageous people continued to challenge the constitutionality of segregation. The National Association for the Advancement of Colored People (NAACP), a multiracial group that had formed in 1909 to combat Jim Crow laws, brought many of these cases to trial. The NAACP enlisted hundreds of lawyers and

THE NAACP

The NAACP formed in 1909 and is still active today. The root philosophy of the NAACP is grounded in a firm belief in integration. The group believes the US Constitution and the democratic ideas of the United States supply the groundwork for a just society.

The group had its roots in the abolitionist movement of the nineteenth century. Its first chairman was the grandson of William Lloyd Garrison, a white abolitionist leader. The group sought an alternative to Booker T. Washington's philosophy of slow economic advancement, seeking instead swift social change. It found white supremacist ideas contrary to the Constitution and resolved to change white racism from within the system, choosing to lobby and bring legal action rather than use more radical approaches such as civil disobedience. By 1938, when the challenge to Plessy would begin in earnest, the NAACP would greatly lessen its lobbying and focus more on court action.

created citizen committees to engage in the battle for equal rights.

In 1913, the NAACP challenged the grandfather clause in Oklahoma in *Guinn v. United States*. Though the US Supreme Court did find the grandfather clause a violation of the Fifteenth Amendment, it made little difference in stopping discrimination at the voting box.

Different from the Citizens' Committee, which challenged segregation outright, the NAACP decided to focus on challenging the equality of public accommodations for blacks and whites. The rationale behind this strategy was that providing separate facilities for blacks that were truly equal would be so costly to the states they would be forced to integrate on their own.

The NAACP also decided to focus on education, where there were great discrepancies in accommodations and funding of white and black public schools. Since the idea of young black and white children sharing the same classroom was hateful to whites in Jim Crow states, the NAACP focused on higher education at first. The idea here was since many adult blacks and whites shared company on a daily basis, sharing a college classroom might not be as objectionable.

The NAACP's challenge to the legality of the *Plessy* decision began in 1938, when NAACP lawyer Thurgood Marshall led the defense in *Missouri ex rel. Gaines v. Canada*. Lloyd Gaines was a black college student who sought admission to the University of Missouri Law School. S. Woodson Canada was the school's registrar. The school rejected Gaines's application and offered to pay his tuition to an out-of-state law school. The

Thurgood Marshall fought many cases on behalf of the NAACP.

Supreme Court ruled that because Missouri provided law school education for whites, it must do so for black citizens as well.

In the 1930s and 1940s, the NAACP was involved in several suits to require equal pay for black teachers, and in 1946, the NAACP won a voter-registration suit. In *Bush v. Board of Education*, begun in 1949, the NAACP won a suit ending the segregation of the New Orleans school system.

These successes were followed by further integration rulings in 1950. That year, Herman Sweatt applied to the University of Texas's all-white law school. Instead of allowing Sweatt to attend classes with other white students, the university created its own underfunded black law school. Marshall and the NAACP sued because the black law school the university had established did not provide the same quality of education accessible to the white students. The US Supreme Court ruled in Sweatt's favor in *Sweatt v. Painter*. In a unanimous decision on June 5, the court found the quality of education between the black and white law schools was overwhelmingly different and that Sweatt should be allowed to enter the university's white law school.

THURGOOD MARSHALL

Thurgood Marshall was one of the top lawyers in the country, black or white. Born in 1908 in Baltimore, Maryland, Marshall attended law school at the all-black Howard University. Marshall became a lawyer for the NAACP and brought many civil rights cases to court. In the 1940s and 1950s, Marshall argued 32 cases before the US Supreme Court and won 29 of them.[5] In 1967, Marshall became the first black justice to serve on the US Supreme Court. He was a strong defender of minority civil rights.

Also that spring, the Supreme Court heard another case led by Marshall and the NAACP, *McLaurin v. Oklahoma Board of Regents of Higher Education.* In this case, George McLaurin, an African American, had been admitted to the University of Oklahoma's doctoral program in education but was not allowed to mingle with his white peers. He could not sit near classmates during lectures and was forced to eat separately from the white students. The Supreme Court, ruling on the same day as the *Sweatt* decision, ruled that the university's policy of separating McLaurin from his peers had detrimental effects on the quality of his education. They ordered the policy be eliminated immediately.

Brown v. Board of Education

Marshall's long-term strategy to end segregation would culminate in *Brown v. Board of Education*. In *Brown*, the focus of the case would involve younger plaintiffs from public grade schools and secondary schools. *Brown* was actually five consolidated cases. Though the cases varied somewhat, they all shared the charge that separate was not equal. The Supreme Court heard *Brown* in 1954 and ruled unanimously on May 17 that schools that were separate could not be equal, even if they were funded equally. The justices found that the states had violated the Fourteenth Amendment, which provided equal

BROWN BEGINS

Similar to many black children of her day, Linda Brown of Topeka, Kansas, had to walk a long distance to attend her public school. Just a few blocks away, however, was a public elementary school open to white students only. Linda's school and the educational materials she was provided with, including books, were far inferior to those available to white children her age. Linda's parents and 11 other families sued in federal court, claiming the black schools were far from equal to the white schools in Topeka. This case, *Brown v. Board of Education*, progressed through the federal courts to the US Supreme Court, consolidating with several similar cases along the way.

protection under the law, and concluded that separate educational facilities were "inherently unequal."[6]

Chief Justice Earl Warren wrote the opinion for the court. In it, he asserted that the *Plessy* decision depended on the idea of white supremacy. Warren cited several social scientists of his day to support his rejection of the idea of white supremacy, overturning the justification of the *Plessy* verdict. Warren also used social science to assert that the act of segregation itself made black students feel inferior and inhibited their ability to learn, saying when segregation is present in schools, especially when supported by law, segregation "had a tendency to [slow] the educational and mental development of negro children and to deprive them of the benefits they would receive in a racially integrated school system."[7]

The *Brown* decision would not take effect immediately, however. In 1955, a year after the original ruling, the court ruled on what would become known as *Brown II*, in which the justices laid out their plan for the implementation of *Brown*. Though the NAACP argued for immediate desegregation, the court worried that would only end in resistance and violence. What the court proposed instead was that desegregation move forward "with all deliberate speed."[8] Attempts to segregate schools did meet with resistance, and twice met with so much violence that the US Army was summoned to enforce integration—in 1957, in Little Rock, Arkansas, and in 1962, in Oxford, Mississippi.

> "Segregation of white and colored children in public schools has a detrimental effect upon the colored children. The impact is greater when it has the sanction of the law, for the policy of separating the races is usually interpreted as denoting the inferiority of the negro group. A sense of inferiority affects the motivation of a child to learn. Segregation with the sanction of law, therefore, has a tendency to [retard] the educational and mental development of negro children and to deprive them of some of the benefits they would receive in a racial[ly] integrated school system."[9]
>
> —*CHIEF JUSTICE EARL WARREN IN THE MAJORITY OPINION FOR* BROWN V. BOARD OF EDUCATION

It was not until 14 years after the *Brown* ruling, in 1968, that the Supreme Court ordered the immediate desegregation of schools. In *Green v. New Kent County*, the court ruled that school boards had the obligation to desegregate schools without delay. The court ruled unanimously. School officials, the court said, had the duty "to take whatever action may be necessary

to create a 'unitary, nonracial system.'"[10] As Justice
William Brennan ordered,

> *School boards . . . operating state-compelled*
> *dual systems were . . . clearly charged with the*
> *affirmative duty to take whatever steps might be*
> *necessary to . . . convert to a [single] system in*
> *which racial discrimination would be eliminated*
> *root and branch. . . .*[11] ∼

Chapter 10

After *Brown*

Approximately six months after Justice Warren urged states to desegregate schools "with all deliberate speed," another monumental event occurred.[1] Though the fight for freedom had been raging for more than a century, many experts have marked this event as the beginning of the civil rights movement. It all started when a woman refused to stand.

On December 1, 1955, Rosa Parks, a 42-year-old resident of Montgomery, Alabama, boarded a city bus on her way home from work. Parks, an African-American woman, worked as a seamstress. She had also worked for the NAACP for many years. The buses in Montgomery were segregated, and

Rosa Parks was arrested for refusing to give up her bus seat to a white passenger.

that day, Parks took a seat in the black section of the bus, just behind the last whites-only row. Soon, the bus became crowded, and the whites-only section was filled to capacity with white riders. At that point, according to bus policy, the driver asked Parks and the other three black passengers to move to the rear of the bus to make more room for white passengers in the front. Without fuss, much as did Plessy so many years before, Parks simply refused. Parks was arrested and found guilty of violating one of Montgomery's Jim Crow ordinances. She promptly appealed her **conviction**, thus challenging the legality of the Jim Crow status quo.

> Back then, we didn't have any civil rights. It was just a matter of survival, of existing from one day to the next. I remember going to sleep as a girl hearing the Klan ride at night and hearing a lynching and being afraid the house would burn down."[2]
>
> —ROSA PARKS REMEMBERING HER CHILDHOOD

Parks's courageous act of civil disobedience was backed up by powerful action from the black

conviction—The process of finding someone guilty.

A FLASHPOINT FOR RACIAL TENSIONS

In the South, racial tension often played out on buses and other forms of public transportation. Jim Crow laws successfully segregated the races in most public places; buses and similar vehicles were an exception in which whites and blacks had to share space. Drivers were given considerable leeway in seating passengers. In Montgomery, bus drivers even carried guns to enforce their seating decisions. As Rosa Parks's lawyer explained, "Virtually every African-American person in Montgomery had some negative experience with the buses. But we had no choice. We had to use the buses for transportation."[3]

community, including a bus boycott. Blacks made up approximately 75 percent of the city bus riders. Black leaders hoped the economic pressure of a bus boycott would inspire the bus company to integrate city buses.

On December 5, 1955, just four days after Parks's refusal and motivated by Parks's arrest, black leaders staged a one-day bus boycott in Montgomery. By the end of the day, some 40,000 riders had boycotted the buses. Though the buses still ran, they ran nearly empty through Montgomery's streets. That evening, boycotters assembled at a local church to vote whether to keep the boycott going.

RESOLVED TO BOYCOTT

On December 5, 1955, four days after Parks's refusal to relinquish her seat to a white man and subsequent arrest, a one-day bus boycott was enacted. The boycott was so successful that, on that evening, a meeting was held to decide if the boycott should continue. The overwhelming answer was yes. A resolution was drawn up to clearly state the purpose of the boycott. In part, it read:

> *Be It Resolved As Follows:*
>
> *1. That the citizens of Montgomery are requesting that every citizen in Montgomery, regardless of race, color or creed, to refrain from riding buses owned . . . by the Montgomery [City] Lines, Incorporated, until some arrangement has been worked out [with] the Montgomery City Lines, Incorporated. . . .*
>
> *Be it further resolved that we have not, . . . we are not, and we have no intentions of using any unlawful means or any intimidation to persuade persons not to ride the Montgomery City Lines buses. However, we call upon your conscience, both moral and spiritual, to give your wholehearted support to this worthy undertaking.*[4]

It was at this meeting that a young pastor from Atlanta, Georgia, stepped into the spotlight. Reverend Martin Luther King Jr. was the new pastor of a local church. The Montgomery Improvement Association was established at that meeting, and the 26-year-old King became its leader. He would soon become the leader of the civil rights movement. That night, he addressed the crowd, saying "If we are wrong, the Constitution of the United States is wrong."[5]

Initially, the demands of boycott leaders did not challenge Jim Crow laws outright. They allowed for separate sections for blacks and whites, but pushed for a middle section between the two where riders could sit on a first-come basis regardless of race. They also asked for courteous treatment of all passengers and called for black drivers to be hired for black bus routes. These demands were rejected, spurring the boycotters to call for the full integration of the buses.

The bus boycott lasted 381 days. Though the boycotters and organizers felt the wrath of racist groups such as the Ku Klux Klan and the White Citizens' Council, they were able to maintain their commitment, developing a car pool system to transport would-be bus passengers. Many people walked long distances rather than ride the bus.

By the end of the boycott, the bus company agreed to the demands of the Montgomery Improvement Association, but the city government insisted the bus company still adhere to the Jim Crow laws, forcing segregation on the buses. In November 1956, the Supreme Court ruled on *Browder v. Gayle*, which challenged the constitutionality of segregated buses. The Supreme Court upheld a lower court's ruling that segregation on buses was illegal, and the buses were ordered to integrate. Thousands began riding the buses again, sitting where they pleased without regard to race.

This change did not pass without resistance, however. Black leader and pastor Ralph David Abernathy had his house and his church bombed. Shots were fired at passing buses as well, and black riders were harassed in many different ways. Members of the civil rights movement still had an uphill battle ahead.

Freedom Rides

Segregation on interstate buses was at issue as well. Though the Supreme Court had ruled against segregation on interstate buses and in stations in 1960 in *Boynton v. Virginia*, the policy continued to thrive throughout the Jim Crow South. Not only were the buses segregated, but also the ticket counters, restaurants, waiting rooms, and restrooms of the bus stations. As on the earlier Montgomery city buses, blacks were expected

DR. MARTIN LUTHER KING JR. SPEAKS

On June 27, 1956, King addressed the 47th annual NAACP convention in San Francisco, California. He spoke not only about the effectiveness of the Montgomery bus boycott but also made clear how the cause in Montgomery was the universal cause of justice:

But you can now see that the one-day protest moved out into an indefinite protest which has lasted now for more than six months. So it is becoming clear now. The history of injustices on the buses has been a long one. . . . But you know there comes a time in this life that people get tired of being trampled over by the iron feet of oppression. . . . The story of Montgomery is the story of fifty thousand Negroes who are tired of oppression and injustice, and who are willing . . . to substitute tired feet for tired souls, and walk and walk and walk until the sagging walls of injustice have been crushed by the battering rams of historical necessity.[6]

to relinquish their seats to whites if the whites-only section was filled.

On May 4, 1961, a group of young people, seven black and six white, all members of the Congress On Racial Equality (CORE), left on two buses traveling from Washington DC to New Orleans, where Plessy had taken his historic ride, to challenge the racist and illegal

135

Jim Crow policies on interstate buses. This journey and those that followed would be called the freedom rides.

Outside Anniston, Alabama, a mob of whites slashed the tires of one bus and set it on fire, initially refusing to let the riders escape the flaming vehicle. On the other bus, the bus driver allowed the mob on the bus, and the mob beat the freedom riders with bats and chains. When they arrived in Birmingham, Alabama, the riders were again violently attacked while the police chief looked on, preventing the police from interfering with the attack. Other freedom rides followed.

On May 20, a group of freedom riders arrived in Montgomery. There they were beaten, though the Alabama governor had assured US president John F. Kennedy the riders would pass unharmed. A rally was held at the First Baptist Church to protest the beatings, and King flew in to address the crowd. Six hundred federal marshals were summoned to protect the riders from further violence, but as the protest went on inside the church, an angry white mob assembled outside. The National Guard was summoned to support the marshals, and the mob was eventually dispersed.

The rides continued, until on September 22, 1961, the Interstate Commerce Commission officially

This freedom ride bus was set on fire in Alabama in May 1961.

prohibited racial discrimination on interstate buses. There is little chance that Homer Plessy, boarding the train on June 7, 1892, could have foreseen the twists and turns his journey would take. From his initial trial to the overturn of the *Plessy* case in the Supreme Court, it would take more than half a century for Plessy's symbolic journey to be resolved. Nor was Plessy the first of his kind: he was one of many from different backgrounds across history to stand up for fundamental human freedoms. And some would say the struggle to end racism and injustice has not ended yet. ∼

Plessy and Ferguson descendants Keith Plessy and Phoebe Ferguson work together today to continue fighting racism.

TIMELINE OF EVENTS AND RULINGS

1857	**March 6**	The US Supreme Court rules in the *Dred Scott v. Missouri* case that blacks are not US citizens.
1863	**March 17**	Homer Plessy is born.
1865	**December 6**	The Thirteenth Amendment to the US Constitution is ratified, making slavery illegal.
1868	**July 9**	The Fourteenth Amendment is ratified, granting citizenship and "equal protection of the laws" to everyone born in the United States.
1890	**July**	Louisiana's Separate Car Act passes, ordering that blacks and whites ride in separate train cars.
1891	**September 1**	The Citizens' Committee to Test the Constitutionality of the Separate Car Act is formed.
1892	**February 24**	Daniel Desdunes tests the Separate Car Act by refusing to leave the whites-only car, but his case is soon dismissed.
	June 7	Plessy is arrested for riding in the whites-only section of a train in New Orleans, Louisiana.
	October 28	Hearings for *Homer Plessy v. The State of Louisiana* begin. Plessy's lawyers ask for the case to be dismissed.
	November 18	Judge Ferguson rules the case should continue; Plessy's lawyers quickly appeal the decision to the Louisiana Supreme Court.

1892	**December 19**	The Louisiana Supreme Court rules against Plessy in *Ex Parte Plessy*.
1893	**February**	The US Supreme Court agrees to hear *Plessy v. Ferguson*, Plessy's case challenging Ferguson's decision to prosecute Plessy.
1896	**April 13**	Plessy's lawyers argue for him before the US Supreme Court.
	May 18	The Supreme Court rules on *Plessy*, finding that "separate but equal" accommodations are constitutional and Plessy's prosecution can continue.
1897	**January 11**	Plessy appears in court, pleads guilty to breaking the Separate Car Act, and pays a $25 fine.
1925	**March 1**	Plessy dies in New Orleans.
1950	**June 5**	The US Supreme Court rules in *Sweatt v. Painter* and *McLaurin v. Oklahoma* that universities must integrate.
1954	**May 17**	The Supreme Court rules in *Brown v. Board of Education* that segregation in public schools is unconstitutional.
1955	**December 1**	Rosa Parks refuses to give up her seat on a bus in Montgomery, Alabama.
	December 5	The boycott of Montgomery buses begins.
1956	**November 13**	The Supreme Court upholds the decision of a lower court in *Browder v. Gayle* that buses must integrate.
1961	**September 22**	Racial discrimination on interstate buses is prohibited by the Interstate Commerce Commission.

GLOSSARY

abolitionist

A person who works to end slavery.

accommodation

The act of compromising or adapting to please others.

caste

A division of society based on wealth, race, employment, or other category.

civil disobedience

A refusal to obey the government or laws in order to protest government action.

emancipation

The act of setting free.

enfranchise

To grant the right to vote.

freedman

A former slave.

indoctrinate

To teach a partisan or prejudiced viewpoint.

integration

The inclusion of people of all races on an equal basis in neighborhoods, schools, parks, or other facilities.

intrastate

Within one state.

lobby

To influence members of the government to support legislation.

lynch

To put to death illegally through mob action.

racism

The belief that a particular race is superior to other races.

ratify

To confirm.

secede

To split away from the Union.

segregation

The separation of one racial group from another or from the rest of society.

subordinate

Lower in rank, class, or position.

veto

To refuse to approve.

white supremacy

The belief that white people are superior to others.

BRIEFS

Petitioner

Homer Plessy

Respondent

Judge John Ferguson

Date of Ruling

May 18, 1896

Summary of Impacts

On June 7, 1892, Homer Plessy took a seat in the whites-only section of a train in New Orleans, Louisiana. Plessy was one-eighth black and very light skinned. He announced to the conductor that he was in fact a person of color. He refused to move to the blacks-only car and was arrested.

Plessy's arrest was orchestrated by the Citizens' Committee to Test the Constitutionality of the Separate Car Act. Passed in 1890, the law required whites and blacks ride in separate cars that were equal in accommodations. The Citizens' Committee sought to initiate a test case, in hopes of appealing the case to the US Supreme Court to challenge the constitutionality of the Separate Car Act.

As the case made its way through the courts, the Separate Car Act was ruled constitutional by a New Orleans court, as well as the Supreme Court of Louisiana. In 1896, the case appeared before the Supreme Court, which upheld the lower courts' ruling. The Separate Car Act was constitutional. Plessy returned to New Orleans, changed his plea to guilty, and paid the required $25 fine.

Though the case was over, the repercussions of the ruling would affect decades of laws. Following the ruling, many states passed "separate but equal" laws that segregated almost all facets of civic life. The *Plessy* verdict was finally overturned in 1954 with the Supreme Court's ruling on *Brown v. Board of Education*.

Quotes

"Legislation is powerless to eradicate racial instincts or to abolish distinctions based upon physical differences, and the attempt to do so can only result in accentuating the difficulties of the present situation. If the civil and political rights of both races be equal, one cannot be inferior to the other civilly or politically. If one race be inferior to the other socially, the Constitution of the United States cannot put them upon the same plane."

—*Justice Henry B. Brown, majority opinion,* Plessy v. Ferguson

"But in view of the Constitution, in the eye of the law, there is in this country no superior, dominant, ruling class of citizens. There is no caste here. Our Constitution is color-blind, and neither knows nor tolerates classes among citizens. In respect of civil rights, all citizens are equal before the law."

—*Justice John Marshall Harlan, dissent,* Plessy v. Ferguson

ADDITIONAL RESOURCES

Selected Bibliography

Fireside, Harvey. *Separate and Unequal: Homer Plessy and the Supreme Court Decision that Legalized Racism*. New York: Carroll & Graf, 2004. Print.

Lofgren, Charles A. *The Plessy Case: A Legal-Historical Interpretation*. New York: Oxford UP, 1987. Print.

Medley, Keith Weldon. *We as Freemen*. Gretna, Louisiana: Pelican, 2003. Print.

Further Readings

Carlisle, Rodney P. *The African Americans*. New York: Facts on File, 2011. Print.

Haskins, Jim. *Separate but Not Equal: The Dream and the Struggle*. New York: Scholastic, 2002. Print.

King, David C. *American Voices: Civil War and Reconstruction*. New York: Wiley, 2003. Print.

Web Links

To learn more about *Plessy v. Ferguson*, visit ABDO Publishing Company online at **www.abdopublishing.com**. Web sites about *Plessy* are featured on our Book Links page. These links are routinely monitored and updated to provide the most current information available.

Places to Visit

Homer Plessy's Grave

Saint Louis Cemetery No. 1

615 Pere Antoine Alley

3421 Esplanade Ave New Orleans, LA 70119

504-525-9585

Take a walking tour of the oldest cemetery in New Orleans and visit Homer Plessy's grave.

The Supreme Court Building

1 First Street, NE, Washington, DC 20543

202-479-3000

http://www.supremecourt.gov/Default.aspx

At the Supreme Court Building, visitors can sit in on oral arguments, attend lectures, tour the building, see exhibitions, and view statues of the chief justices.

SOURCE NOTES

Chapter 1. A Fateful Ride

1. Harvey Fireside. *Separate and Unequal: Homer Plessy and the Supreme Court Decision that Legalized Racism*. New York: Carroll & Graf, 2004. Print. 1.

2. Keith Weldon Medley. *We as Freemen*. Gretna, LA: Pelican, 2003. Print. 89.

3. Charles A. Lofgren. *The Plessy Case: A Legal-Historical Interpretation*. New York: Oxford UP, 1987. Print. 16.

Chapter 2. Slavery and the Civil War

1. Frederick Douglass. *Biographies: Narrative of the Life, My Bondage and My Freedom, Life and Times*. New York: Library of America, 1994. 420. *Google Book Search*. Web. 19 Apr. 2012.

2. "DRED SCOTT v. SANDFORD, 60 U.S. 393 (1856)." *FindLaw*. FindLaw, n.d. Web. 19 Apr. 2012.

3. Abraham Lincoln. "A Letter from President Lincoln; Reply to Horace Greeley. Slavery and the Union; The Restoration of the Union the Paramount Object." *New York Times*. New York Times, 22 Aug. 1862. Web. 19 Apr. 2012.

4. "Featured Document: The Emancipation Proclamation." *National Archives and Records Administration*. National Archives and Records Administration, n.d. Web. 8 Nov. 2011.

5. Harvey Fireside. *Separate and Unequal: Homer Plessy and the Supreme Court Decision that Legalized Racism*. New York: Carroll & Graf, 2004. Print. 33.

6. "The Constitution of the United States: Amendments 11–27." *National Archives and Records Administration*. National Archives and Records Administration, n.d. Web. 8 Nov. 2011.

7. Ibid.

8. Ibid.

Chapter 3. The Black Codes and Reconstruction

1. "State by State: Special Features—Reconstruction Timeline: 1863–1866." *American Experience: Reconstruction—The Second Civil War.* PBS Online/WGBH Boston, n.d. Web. 19 Apr. 2012.

2. Keith Weldon Medley. *We as Freemen.* Gretna, LA: Pelican, 2003. Print. 83.

Chapter 4. Reconstruction Ends

1. W. E. B. Du Bois. *Black Reconstruction in America 1860–1880.* New York: Simon, 1999. 30. *Google Book Search.* Web. 19 Apr. 2011.

2. "Black Legislators: Primary Sources—Laws Fail to Protect Us." *American Experience: Reconstruction—The Second Civil War.* PBS Online/WGBH Boston, n.d. Web. 19 Apr. 2012.

3. "The Battle of Liberty Place." *KnowLA Encyclopedia of Louisiana.* Louisiana Endowment for the Humanities, 2010. Web. 19 Apr. 2011.

4. Steven Mintz. "Reconstruction: Redemption." *Digital History.* Digital History, n.d. Web. 13 Nov. 2011.

5. Charles A. Lofgren. *The Plessy Case: A Legal-Historical Interpretation.* New York: Oxford UP, 1987. Print. 21.

6. Ibid. 120.

Chapter 5. Fighting Segregation in New Orleans

1. Henry David Thoreau. "Civil Disobedience—Part 2 of 3." *thoreau.eserver.org.* Thoreau Reader, n.d. Web. 19 Apr. 2012.

2. Keith Weldon Medley. *We as Freemen.* Gretna, LA: Pelican, 2003. Print. 20–21.

3. Ibid. 97.

4. Otto H. Olsen, ed. *The Thin Disguise: Plessy v. Ferguson.* New York: Humanities, 1967. Print. 53.

5. Ibid. 55.

6. Keith Weldon Medley. *We as Freemen.* Gretna, LA: Pelican, 2003. Print. 161.

Chapter 6. The *Plessy* Case Begins

1. Harvey Fireside. *Separate and Unequal: Homer Plessy and the Supreme Court Decision that Legalized Racism*. New York: Carroll & Graf, 2004. Print. 5.

2. Ibid. 121.

3. Charles A. Lofgren. *The Plessy Case: A Legal-Historical Interpretation*. New York: Oxford UP, 1987. Print. 46.

4. Harvey Fireside. *Separate and Unequal: Homer Plessy and the Supreme Court Decision that Legalized Racism*. New York: Carroll & Graf, 2004. Print. 122–123.

5. Charles A. Lofgren. *The Plessy Case: A Legal-Historical Interpretation*. New York: Oxford UP, 1987. Print. 46.

6. Ibid.

7. Harvey Fireside. *Separate and Unequal: Homer Plessy and the Supreme Court Decision that Legalized Racism*. New York: Carroll & Graf, 2004. Print. 138.

8. Charles A. Lofgren. *The Plessy Case: A Legal-Historical Interpretation*. New York: Oxford UP, 1987. Print. 51.

9. Harvey Fireside. *Separate and Unequal: Homer Plessy and the Supreme Court Decision that Legalized Racism*. New York: Carroll & Graf, 2004. Print. 140.

10. Charles A. Lofgren. *The Plessy Case: A Legal-Historical Interpretation*. New York: Oxford UP, 1987. Print. 53.

11. Keith Weldon Medley. *We as Freemen*. Gretna, LA: Pelican, 2003. Print. 167–168.

12. Harvey Fireside. *Separate and Unequal: Homer Plessy and the Supreme Court Decision that Legalized Racism*. New York: Carroll & Graf, 2004. Print. 141.

Chapter 7. A Changing Society

1. Keith Weldon Medley. *We as Freemen*. Gretna, LA: Pelican, 2003. Print. 185.

2. Ibid. 175.

3. Ibid. 175–177.

4. Ibid. 178.

5. Otto H. Olsen. "Albion W. Tourgée and Negro Militants of the 1890s: A Documentary Selection." *Science & Society* 28.2 (Spring 1964): 198. *JSTOR*. Web. 19 Apr. 2012.

6. Keith Weldon Medley. *We as Freemen*. Gretna, LA: Pelican, 2003. Print. 189.

7. Ibid. 192.

Chapter 8. The Supreme Court

1. Keith Weldon Medley. *We as Freemen*. Gretna, LA: Pelican, 2003. Print. 200–201.

2. "*Plessy v. Ferguson*, 163 U.S. 537 (1896)." *Legal Information Institute*. Cornell University Law School, n.d. Web. 19 Apr. 2012.

3. Ibid.

4. Ibid.

5. Ibid.

6. Ibid.

7. Lawrence M. Friedman. *A History of American Law*. 3rd ed. New York: Simon, 2005. 286. *Google Book Search*. Web. 19 Apr. 2012.

8. "*Plessy v. Ferguson*, 163 U.S. 537 (1896)." *Legal Information Institute*. Cornell University Law School, n.d. Web. 19 Apr. 2012.

Chapter 9. After *Plessy*

1. Keith Weldon Medley. *We as Freemen*. Gretna, LA: Pelican, 2003. Print. 206.

2. Ibid. 209–210.

3. Ibid. 210.

4. Hanes Walton. *Invisible Politics: Black Political Behavior*. Albany, NY: SUNY, 1985. 86. *Google Book Search*. Web. 19 Apr. 2012.

5. "Supreme Court History: Expanding Civil Rights— Biographies of the Robes: Thurgood Marshall." *The Supreme Court*. Educational Broadcasting Corp., 2007. Web. 19 Apr. 2012.

6. "*Brown v. Board of Education of Topeka*, 37 U.S. 483 (1954). *Legal Information Institute*. Cornell University Law School, n.d. Web. 19 Apr. 2012.

7. Ibid.

8. "*Brown v. Board of Education* (II)." *The Oyez Project*. IIT Chicago-Kent College of Law, n.d. Web. 19 Apr. 2012.

9. "*Brown v. Board of Education of Topeka*, 37 U.S. 483 (1954). *Legal Information Institute*. Cornell University Law School, n.d. Web. 19 Apr. 2012.

10. "*Green v. County School Board of New Kent County*, 391 U.S. 430 (1968)." *Legal Information Institute*. Cornell University Law School, n.d. Web. 19 Apr. 2012.

11. Ibid.

Chapter 10. After *Brown*

1. "*Brown v. Board of Education* (II)." *The Oyez Project.* IIT Chicago-Kent College of Law, n.d. Web. 19 Apr. 2012.

2. Marney Rich. "Rosa Parks: 'I Was Just One of Many Who Fought for Freedom.'" *Chicago Tribune.* Chicago Tribune, 3 Apr. 1988. Web. 19 Apr. 2012.

3. "Rosa Parks Bus: The Story behind the Bus." *The Henry Ford.* The Henry Ford, 2002. Web. 19 Apr. 2012.

4. "5 December 1955, MIA Mass Meeting at Holt Street Baptist Church, Montgomery, Ala." *Martin Luther King Jr. and the Global Freedom Struggle.* The Martin Luther King Jr. Research and Education Institute, n.d. Web. 19 Apr. 2012.

5. "The Story of the Movement: The Montgomery Bus Boycott." *American Experience: Eyes on the Prize.* PBS Online/WGBH Boston, n.d. Web. 19 Apr. 2012.

6. "The Montgomery Story." *The Papers of Martin Luther King Jr.: Volume 3: Birth of a New Age, December 1955–December 1956.* The Martin Luther King Jr. Research and Education Institute, n.d. Web. 19 Apr. 2012.

INDEX

R

racism, 11, 20, 48–49, 50,
62, 91, 94, 96, 119, 138
See also prejudice; white
supremacy
Reconstruction Acts, 36,
38–40, 49
Reconstruction era, 14, 15,
32–41, 49, 62, 68, 93, 95,
100, 103
Republicans, 34, 37, 40, 45,
46, 47, 50, 72, 91
Radical Republicans,
36–37
Rochon, Victor, 65

S

Sanford, John, 23
Scott, Dred, 21–23
segregation, 14, 15, 16, 49,
52, 54–55, 61, 75, 84–85,
87, 91, 95–96, 101,
111–112, 115–116, 118,
120, 122, 124–126, 128,
131, 134
See also Jim Crow laws;
separate-but-equal policies
separate-but-equal policies,
12, 13, 49, 51–52, 54–57,
63, 83–84, 87, 91, 106,
116, 118, 120, 124–125

See also Jim Crow laws;
segregation
Separate Car Act, 12–13,
58, 62–72, 76–77, 79–83,
86, 87, 96, 105–109,
111–112, 116
Seymour, Horatio, 40
Shiras, George, Jr., 103
slave codes, 35
slavery, 11, 14, 18–31, 34,
37, 39, 43, 66, 74, 75, 98,
103, 107, 109
Supreme Court, US, 15,
22–23, 52, 75, 78, 84,
87, 88, 90, 92, 95, 97,
100–101, 102–112, 114,
119, 122–124, 126, 134,
137
Sweatt v. Painter, 122–123

T

Taney, Roger B., 23–24
Thirteenth Amendment, 18,
28–29, 71, 75, 78–79,
82–83, 106–107
Tourgée, Albion, 68–69,
72–73, 78–82, 87, 92–93,
94, 96, 102, 104–105,
114–115

U

Unification Movement, 14,
39, 97

About the Author

David Cates is an author and teacher. He has taught English in diverse locations around the world, including India, Nepal, and Japan. David lives in Georgia with his wife and two children. This is his third book.

About the Content Consultant

Professor Margalynne Armstrong was born and raised in Chicago. She majored in English at Earlham College and received her law degree from the University of California–Berkeley. She joined the Santa Clara University faculty in 1987.